STATEMENT ON RACE

ASHLEY MONTAGU

Statement on Race

AN ANNOTATED ELABORATION AND EXPOSITION
OF THE FOUR STATEMENTS ON RACE ISSUED BY
THE UNITED NATIONS EDUCATIONAL, SCIENTIFIC,
AND CULTURAL ORGANIZATION

THIRD EDITION

OXFORD UNIVERSITY PRESS
London   Oxford   New York
1972

London   Oxford   New York
Glasgow   Toronto   Melbourne   Wellington
Cape Town   Ibadan   Nairobi   Dar Es Salaam   Lusaka   Addis Ababa
Delhi   Bombay   Calcutta   Madras   Karachi   Lahore   Dacca
Kuala Lumpur   Singapore   Hong Kong   Tokyo

FIRST EDITION published by Henry Schuman, Inc., 1951
SECOND EDITION published by Henry Schuman, Inc., 1953
THIRD EDITION published by Oxford University Press, Inc., 1972
First issued as an Oxford University Press paperback, 1972

Grateful acknowledgment is made for permission to reprint
the four Statements on Race prepared by UNESCO and reproduced
with its permission—UNESCO 1969

Printed in the United States of America

Dedicated to the Memory of

GEORGE BIDGOOD

Beloved Schoolmaster

417613

Contents

PREFACE *to the Third Edition*

The first edition of this work was originally published in 1951 in order to clarify for the reader the foundations upon which the first UNESCO Statement on Race, issued in 1950, was based. A second edition was published early in 1953; this differed from the first only in that it made available the second Statement on Race issued by UNESCO in 1952. Since that time two additional statements on race have been issued by UNESCO. Because the earlier editions of this book appeared to serve a useful purpose it was thought that a volume making all four statements available, together with an extended discussion of them, would be helpful to many readers, especially those actively engaged in attempting to come to grips with the problems of race and race relations.

The whole work has been thoroughly revised, and both the references and the annotated list of books and pamphlets on race have been entirely replaced by new ones.

The method adopted in the first is followed in the present edition, namely, each paragraph of the fourth Statement— since the second and third Statements are self-explanatory and require no further exposition—receives separate discussion and annotation.

It is hoped that the book will serve as a whetstone upon which the reader may sharpen his wits and his understanding of the nature of race, race relations, and racism, and that it will be helpful to him in assisting to bring about those necessary changes in the troublesome problem-area of race relations that are so long overdue.

I am obliged to UNESCO for permission to reprint the four Statements on Race. The commentary on these Statements is, however, entirely my own, and UNESCO is not to be held in any way responsible for it.

A.M.

Princeton, N.J.
22 November 1971

PREFACE *to the First Edition*

In the decade just passed more than six million human beings lost their lives because it was alleged they belonged to an inferior race. The horrible corollary to this barbarism is that it rested on a scientifically untenable premise. On this the scientists of the world are agreed. And through an agency of the United Nations a group of them have gone on record to clarify the whole concept of race.

On July 18, 1950, UNESCO (United Nations Educational, Scientific and Cultural Organization) issued a Statement by Experts on Race Problems. Its consequences should be of truly universal importance, for it effectively demolishes the myth that race determines mental aptitude, temperament, or social habits.

Parts of this Statement were published in the press throughout the world, and the whole of it has appeared in four or five journals. There have been, however, many requests for an interpretative edition of the Statement, which would amplify each paragraph and set forth some of the facts and findings upon which it is based. Since I was the member of the Committee, responsible for the original draft of the Statement, who was called upon to edit it into its final form, the publisher suggested that I undertake the present volume. The project appealed to me because of the obvious value of such a volume, the enlarged circulation it would give to the Statement, and the opportunity to put the meanings contained in its unavoidably compact paragraphs, into as plain English as possible.

It is hoped that the book will appeal to the general reader, to the student, to leaders of discussion groups, and above all to teachers in the schools and colleges. It seeks to provide them with a compact, clear, and authoritative summary of the facts about race, so urgently needed in our time.

To increase the usefulness of the book I have added a select, annotated list of books and pamphlets on the subject. I have also added the United Nations *Universal Declaration of Human Rights*.

The scientists named below were good enough to read this book in manuscript. Their criticisms and suggestions were of great value in the final shaping of the book and I wish, herewith, to express my thanks to them, and at the same time to absolve them from any remaining faults from which the book may suffer.

Professor William C. Boyd, Department of Biochemistry, Boston University Medical School; Mr. Frederick Briggs, Interscience Foundation, New York; Professor Hadley Cantril, Department of Psychology, Princeton University; Professor Carleton S. Coon, University Museum, University of Pennsylvania; Professor Theodosius Dobzhansky, Department of Zoology, Columbia University; Dr. Lawrence K. Frank, Director of the Caroline Zachry Institute of Human Development, New York; Professor Earnest A. Hooton, Department of Anthropology, Harvard University; Professor Wilton M. Krogman, Graduate School of Medicine, University of Pennsylvania; Professor Ralph Linton, Department of Anthropology, Yale University; Dr. Margaret Mead, Department of Anthropology, American Museum of Natural History, New York; and Dr. Alfred Métraux, Division for the Study of Race Problems, UNESCO, Paris.

A.M.

Department of Anthropology,
Rutgers University,
New Brunswick, N. J.
15 January 1951.

PREFACE *to the Second Edition*

The second edition of this book has been enlarged to include a *Statement on Race* and *Race Differences by Physical Anthropologists and Geneticists.* The basic version of this Statement was drawn up at the Paris headquarters of UNESCO, 4-8 June 1951, and subsequently revised. It is published by UNESCO, and in this book, as of September 1952. It will be found on pages 137-147. Also appended is an account of the origin of the 1952 Statement and a list of those who participated in its drafting.

A.M.

Princeton, N. J.
15 September 1952

STATEMENT ON RACE

The Story of UNESCO'S FIRST STATEMENT ON RACE PROBLEMS

During the Fourth General Conference of UNESCO (United Nations Educational, Scientific and Cultural Organization) a resolution was approved calling upon its Director-General

1. To collect scientific materials concerning problems of race;
2. To give wide diffusion to the scientific information collected;
3. To prepare an educational campaign based on this information.

The Director-General of UNESCO, Dr. Jaime Torres-Bodet of Mexico, is a distinguished poet. And poets, said Shelley, are the unacknowledged legislators of the world. To that rule—if it be a rule—the Director-General of UNESCO is a happy exception, for he is an acknowledged leader in helping to make the acknowledged laws which may someday inform the conduct of all mankind.

The head of the Social Sciences Department of UNESCO in 1949 was the distinguished Brazilian anthropologist Dr. Arthur Ramos, who was deeply interested in racial problems. Consequently, it was to him and his Department that Dr. Torres-Bodet assigned the task of carrying out the above resolution.

His first step was to call together a committee of experts in the fields of physical anthropology, sociology, social psychology, and ethnology. Their function was to draw up a preliminary definition of race, in conformity with the findings of these sciences.

In October 1949 Dr. Ramos issued an invitation to ten scientists to serve on such a committee, to meet at UNESCO headquarters in Paris on the 12th, 13th, and 14th of December 1949. The following scientists, all of whom accepted, were invited to serve on what came to be designated the Committee of Experts on Race Problems:

Ernest Beaglehole, Professor of Anthropology and Psychology, Victoria University College, New Zealand

Juan Comas, Professor of Anthropology, Escuela Nacional Normal Superior, Liverpool, Mexico, D.F.

Jan Czeckanowski, Professor of Anthropology, University of Lwow, Poland

Franklin Frazier, Professor of Sociology, Howard University, Washington, D.C., United States of America

Morris Ginsberg, Professor of Sociology, University of London, United Kingdom

Humayun Kabir, Joint Secretary, Ministry of Education, New Delhi, India

Claude Lévi-Strauss, Professor of Anthropology, Sorbonne, Paris, France

Ashley Montagu, Professor of Anthropology, Rutgers University, New Brunswick, New Jersey, United States of America

L. A. Costa Pinto, Professor of Anthropology, University of Rio de Janeiro, Brazil

Joseph Sköld, University of Stockholm, Sweden

It is sad to have to record that shortly after the letters of invitation were sent out Dr. Ramos died. In him UNESCO lost an able and devoted servant, and the world of science, a distinguished investigator. Fortunately, Professor Robert C. Angell, on leave from the University of Michigan's Department of

Sociology, had been working closely with Dr. Ramos. He was immediately appointed acting head of the Department of Social Sciences. It was Professor Angell who carried on the further organization of the Committee. He discharged this sudden and heavy responsibility with admirable charm and efficiency. That, from beginning to end, the work ran without a hitch and on schedule, was largely due to the valiant labors of Professor Angell and his staff.

It is the constitutional purpose of UNESCO to harness the forces of education, science, and culture in order to contribute to peace, security, and international understanding by international collaboration.

Article 1 of UNESCO's Constitution states: "The purpose of the Organization is to contribute to peace and security by promoting collaboration among the nations through education, science and culture" by ". . . advancing the mutual knowledge and understanding of peoples, through all means of mass communication." The preamble to the Constitution states that UNESCO was being created "for the purpose of advancing . . . the objectives of international peace *and the common welfare of mankind.*"

It is in fulfillment of these purposes that the resolution at the Fourth Conference was passed and the Committee of Experts on race problems was brought together.

Unfortunately, illness prevented Professor Czeckanowski of Poland and Professor Sköld of Sweden from attending the meetings of the Committee. Of the two United Nations observers, Mr. E. Lawson and Maître Samuel Spanien, only the former was able to attend the meetings.

Representing UNESCO were Professor R. C. Angell of the United States of America, Professor J. R. Xirau exile of Spain resident in France, and Professor P. de Bie of Belgium.

Thus, there were present at the meetings of the Committee twelve persons from eight different nations. All were present at the opening meeting of the Committee on Monday morning, December 12, 1949.

The gathering took place in Unesco House, on the Avenue Kléber, one of the twelve beautiful avenues radiating from the Arc de Triomphe. Less than five years before this house had been the headquarters of the German military during the occupation of Paris. Only if our deliberations had taken place at Auschwitz or Dachau could there have been a more fitting environment to impress upon the Committee members the immense significance of their work.

Our conference room was a large, square-shaped, high-ceilinged room with the usual green baize-covered conference tables arranged in a hollow square. Large white cards bearing our names in black print assigned our places. Professor R. C. Angell (United States) welcomed us on behalf of UNESCO and outlined what it was that UNESCO wished us to consider. Professor Franklin Frazier (United States) was then elected chairman and myself *rapporteur* (reporter).

By the end of the first day's deliberations the Committee had roughed out the general structure of the Statement on Race. This was prepared as a first draft. During the following two days the contents of this draft were thoroughly discussed. It was gone over word by word, sentence by sentence, and paragraph by paragraph. Every statement was microscopically viewed and discussed. Every member of the Committee, together with the U.N. and UNESCO representatives, worked hard to eliminate weak and debatable points, to search out "holes" and doubtful statements. These proved to be gratifyingly few. When finally we got the Statement into shape, agreement on all points was complete, and by the end of the third and last session all members of the Committee were able to sign the Statement without any reservations.

The Statement was then sent by Professor Angell to a number of scientists representing the fields of genetics, general biology, social psychology, sociology, and economics, among them:

Professor Julian Huxley, biologist and first Director-General of UNESCO (United Kingdom)

Dr. Joseph Needham, biochemist and humanist, reader in Biochemistry, Cambridge University (United Kingdom)

Professor L. C. Dunn, geneticist, Department of Zoology, Columbia University, New York (United States)

Professor Theodosius Dobzhansky, geneticist, Department of Zoology, Columbia University, New York (United States)

Professor Otto Klineberg, social psychologist, Department of Psychology, Columbia University, New York (United States)

Professor Gunnar Dahlberg, geneticist, The State Institute for Human Genetics and Race Biology, University of Uppsala (Sweden)

Professor Gunnar Myrdal, economist and sociologist, Department of Economics, University of Stockholm (Sweden), Executive Secretary, Economic Commission for Europe, United Nations, Geneva, Switzerland

The valuable criticisms and suggestions made by these scientists helped to lend greater strength to the Statement. They were sent to Professor Angell and by him transmitted to me, as *rapporteur* and editor of the Committee, for consideration. Most of the suggestions were adopted in what constituted a third draft of the statement—the first being the working draft originally drawn, and the second the one approved by the Committee of Experts at Paris on 14 December, 1949.

Copies of the third draft were then sent to the following scientists in the fields of genetics, general biology, social psychology, sociology, and anthropology, and experts in labor-management relations:

Professor R. C. Angell, sociologist, Department of Sociology, University of Michigan, Ann Arbor (United States), and Department of Social Sciences, UNESCO

Professor Hadley Cantril, social psychologist, Department of Psychology, Princeton University (United States)

Professor Edwin G. Conklin, biologist, Department of Zoology, Princeton University (United States)

Professor Theodosius Dobzhansky, geneticist, Department of Zoology, Columbia University, New York (United States)

Professor L. C. Dunn, geneticist, Department of Zoology, Columbia University, New York (United States)

Professor Donald Hager, anthropologist, Department of Economics and Social Institutions, Princeton University (United States)

Professor Julian Huxley, biologist, and first Director-General of UNESCO (United Kingdom)

Professor Otto Klineberg, social psychologist, Department of Psychology, Columbia University (United States)

Professor Wilbert Moore, sociologist, Department of Economics and Social Institutions, Princeton University (United States)

Professor H. J. Muller, geneticist, Department of Zoology, Indiana University, Bloomington (United States)

Professor Curt Stern, geneticist, Department of Zoology, University of California, Berkeley (United States)

I

Statement on race

PARIS, July 1950

1. Scientists have reached general agreement in recognizing that mankind is one: that all men belong to the same species, *Homo sapiens*. It is further generally agreed among scientists that all men are probably derived from the same common stock; and that such differences as exist between different groups of mankind are due to the operation of evolutionary factors of differentiation such as isolation, the drift and random fixation of the material particles which control heredity (the genes), changes in the structure of these particles, hybridization, and natural selection. In these ways groups have arisen of varying stability and degree of differentiation which have been classified in different ways for different purposes.

2. From the biological standpoint, the species *Homo sapiens* is made up of a number of populations, each one of which differs from the others in the frequency of one or more genes. Such genes, responsible for the hereditary differences between men, are always few when compared to the whole genetic constitution of man and to the vast number of genes common to all human beings regardless of the population to which they belong. This means that the likenesses among men are far greater than their differences.

3. A race, from the biological standpoint, may therefore be

7

defined as one of the group of populations constituting the species *Homo sapiens*. These populations are capable of inter-breeding with one another but, by virtue of the isolating barriers which in the past kept them more or less separated, exhibit certain physical differences as a result of their somewhat different biological histories. These represent variations, as it were, on a common theme.

4. In short, the term "race" designates a group or population characterized by some concentrations, relative as to frequency and distribution, of hereditary particles (genes) or physical characters, which appear, fluctuate, and often disappear in the course of time by reason of geographic and/or cultural isolation. The varying manifestations of these traits in different populations are perceived in different ways by each group. What is perceived is largely preconceived, so that each group arbitrarily tends to misinterpret the variability which occurs as a fundamental difference which separates that group from all others.

5. These are the scientific facts. Unfortunately, however, when most people use the term "race" they do not do so in the sense above defined. To most people, a race is any group of people whom they choose to describe as a race. Thus, many national, religious, geographic, linguistic or cultural groups have, in such loose usage, been called "race," when obviously Americans are not a race, nor are Englishmen, nor Frenchmen, nor any other national group. Catholics, Protestants, Moslems, and Jews are not races, nor are groups who speak English or any other language thereby definable as a race; people who live in Iceland or England or India are not races; nor are people who are culturally Turkish or Chinese or the like thereby describable as races.

6. National, religious, geographic, linguistic and cultural groups do not necessarily coincide with racial groups: and the cultural traits of such groups have no demonstrated genetic connexion with racial traits. Because serious errors of this kind are habitually committed when the term "race" is used in pop-

ular parlance, it would be better when speaking of human races to drop the term "race" altogether and speak of ethnic groups.

7. Now, what has the scientist to say about the groups of mankind which may be recognized at the present time? Human races can be and have been differently classified by different anthropologists, but at the present time most anthropologists agree on classifying the greater part of the present-day mankind into three major divisions as follows: (a) the Mongoloid division; (b) the Negroid division; and (c) the Caucasoid division. The biological processes which the classifier has here embalmed, as it were, are dynamic, not static. These divisions were not the same in the past as they are at present, and there is every reason to believe that they will change in the future.

8. Many sub-groups or ethnic groups within these divisions have been described. There is no general agreement upon their number, and in any event most ethnic groups have not yet been either studied or described by the physical anthropologists.

9. Whatever classification the anthropologist makes of man, he never includes mental characteristics as part of those classifications. It is now generally recognized that intelligence tests do not in themselves enable us to differentiate safely between what is due to innate capacity and what is the result of environmental influences, training and education. Wherever it has been possible to make allowances for differences in environmental opportunities, the tests have shown essential similarity in mental characters among all human groups. In short, given similar degrees of cultural opportunity to realize their potentialities, the average achievement of the members of each ethnic group is about the same. The scientific investigations of recent years fully support the dictum of Confucius (551-478 B.C.): "Men's natures are alike; it is their habits that carry them far apart."

10. The scientific material available to us at present does not justify the conclusion that inherited genetic differences are a major factor in producing the differences between the cultures and cultural achievements of different peoples or groups. It

does indicate, however, that the history of the cultural experience which each group has undergone is the major factor in explaining such differences. The one trait which above all others has been at a premium in the evolution of men's mental characters has been educability, plasticity. This is a trait which all human beings possess. It is indeed, a species character of *Homo sapiens*.

11. So far as temperament is concerned, there is no definite evidence that there exist inborn differences betwen human groups. There is evidence that whatever group differences of the kind there might be are greatly overridden by the individual differences, and by the differences springing from environmental factors.

12. As for personality and character, these may be considered raceless. In every human group a rich variety of personality and character types will be found, and there is no reason for believing that any human group is richer than any other in these respects.

13. With respect to race mixture, the evidence points unequivocally to the fact that this has been going on from the earliest times. Indeed, one of the chief processes of race formation and race extinction or absorption is by means of hybridization between races or ethnic groups. Furthermore, no convincing evidence has been adduced that race mixture of itself produces biologically bad effects. Statements that human hybrids frequently show undesirable traits, both physically and mentally, physical disharmonies and mental degeneracies, are not supported by the facts. There is, therefore, no biological justification for prohibiting intermarriage between persons of different ethnic groups.

14. The biological fact of race and the myth of "race" should be distinguished. For all practical social purposes "race" is not so much a biological phenomenon as a social myth. The myth of "race" has created an enormous amount of human and social damage. In recent years it has taken a heavy toll in human lives and caused untold suffering. It still prevents the normal

development of millions of human beings and deprives civilization of the effective co-operation of productive minds. The biological differences between ethnic groups should be disregarded from the standpoint of social acceptance and social action. The unity of mankind from both the biological and social viewpoints is the main thing. To recognize this and to act accordingly is the first requirement of modern man. It is but to recognize what a great biologist wrote in 1875: "As man advances in civilization, and small tribes are united into larger communities, the simplest reason would tell each individual that he ought to extend his social instincts and sympathies to all the members of the same nation, though personally unknown to him. This point being once reached, there is only an artificial barrier to prevent his sympathies extending to the men of all nations and races." These are the words of Charles Darwin in *The Descent of Man* (2nd ed., 1875, p. 187-8). And, indeed, the whole of human history shows that a co-operative spirit is not only natural to men, but more deeply rooted than any self-seeking tendencies. If this were not so we should not see the growth of integration and organization of his communities which the centuries and the millenniums plainly exhibit.

15. We now have to consider the bearing of these statements on the problem of human equality. It must be asserted with the utmost emphasis that equality as an ethical principle in no way depends upon the assertion that human beings are in fact equal in endowment. Obviously individuals in all ethnic groups vary greatly among themselves in endowment. Nevertheless, the characteristics in which human groups differ from one another are often exaggerated and used as a basis for questioning the validity of equality in the ethical sense. For this purpose we have thought it worth while to set out in a formal manner what is at present scientifically established concerning individual and group differences.

(a) In matters of race, the only characteristics which anthropologists can effectively use as a basis for classifications are physical and physiological.

(b) According to present knowledge there is no proof that the groups of mankind differ in their innate mental characteristics, whether in respect of intelligence or temperament. The scientific evidence indicates that the range of mental capacities in all ethnic groups is much the same.

(c) Historical and sociological studies support the view that genetic differences are not of importance in determining the social and cultural differences between different groups of *Homo sapiens,* and that the social and cultural changes in different groups have, in the main, been independent of changes in inborn constitution. Vast social changes have occurred which were not in any way connected with changes in racial type.

(d) There is no evidence that race mixture as such produces bad results from the biological point of view. The social results of race mixture whether for good or ill are to be traced to social factors.

(e) All normal human beings are capable of learning to share in a common life, to understand the nature of mutual service and reciprocity, and to respect social obligations and contracts. Such biological differences as exist between members of different ethnic groups have no relevance to problems of social and political organization, moral life and communication between human beings.

Lastly, biological studies lend support to the ethic of universal brotherhood; for man is born with drives toward co-operation, and unless these drives are satisfied, men and nations alike fall ill. Man is born a social being who can reach his fullest development only through interaction with his fellows. The denial at any point of this social bond between men and man brings with it disintegration. In this sense, every man is his brother's keeper. For every man is a piece of the continent, a part of the main, because he is involved in mankind.

Original statement drafted at Unesco House, Paris, by the following experts:

Professor Ernest Beaglehole (New Zealand);
Professor Juan Comas (Mexico);
Professor L. A. Costa Pinto (Brazil);
Professor Franklin Frazier (United States of America);
Professor Morris Ginsberg (United Kingdom);
Dr. Humayun Kabir (India);
Professor Claude Lévi-Strauss (France);
Professor Ashley Montagu (United States of America) (rapporteur).

Text revised by Professor Ashley Montagu, after criticism submitted by Professors Hadley Cantril, E. G. Conklin, Gunnar Dahlberg, Theodosius Dobzhansky, L. C. Dunn, Donald Hager, Julian S. Huxley, Otto Klineberg, Wilbert Moore, H. J. Muller, Gunnar Myrdal, Joseph Needham, Curt Stern.

PARAGRAPH 1

Scientists have reached general agreement in recognizing that mankind is one: that all men belong to the same species, Homo sapiens. It is further generally agreed among scientists that all men are probably derived from the same common stock; and that such differences as exist between different groups of mankind are due to the operation of evolutionary factors of differentiation such as isolation, the drift and random fixation of the material particles which control heredity (the genes), changes in the structure of these particles, hybridization, and natural selection. In these ways groups have arisen of varying stability and degree of differentiation which have been classified in different ways for different purposes.

*S cientists have reached general agreement in recogniz-
ing that mankind is one: that all men belong to the
same species,* Homo sapiens. The unity of mankind was
recognized by the founder of systematic biology, Carolus
Linnaeus (Carl Linné, 1707-1778), who gave mankind the
name *Homo sapiens* in 1758.[1] The name *Homo sapiens*
means literally "Man the Wise," which as Oscar Wilde
wittily remarked is perhaps the most premature oafishly
arrogant definition ever offered of any species! In the
nineteenth century there were several scientists who chal-
lenged the conception of the unity of mankind, but their
position proved untenable. In his famous book, *The Descent of Man* (1871), Charles Darwin (1809-1882) summed
up the best, and general, scientific opinion on the subject
in the following words:

"Although the existing races of man differ in many respects, as in colour, hair, shape of skull, proportions of the
body, &c., yet if their whole structure be taken into consideration they are found to resemble each other closely
in a multitude of points. Many of these are of so unim-

15

portant or of so singular a nature, that it is extremely improbable that they should have been independently acquired by aboriginally distinct species or races. The same remark holds good with equal or greater force with respect to the numerous points of mental similarity between the most distinct races of man."[2]

"But the most weighty of all the arguments," says Darwin, "against treating the races of man as distinct species, is that they graduate into each other, independently in many cases, as far as we can judge, of their having intercrossed."[3] And finally, he writes, "As it is improbable that the numerous and unimportant points of resemblance between the several races of man in bodily structure and mental faculties (I do not here refer to similar customs) should all have been independently acquired, they must have been inherited from progenitors who had these same characters."[4]

Since Darwin wrote these words the subject has been reviewed many times by scientists, and apart from a few extraordinary exceptions,[5] Darwin's views on the unity of mankind have been unanimously supported. Let us hear what a most distinguished writer has to say on the subject. He is one of the world's most knowledgeable physical anthropologists, Professor W. E. Le Gros Clark, until recently, head of the School of Anatomy at Oxford University, England. Professor Le Gros Clark points out that "from the purely anatomical point of view, there are already available certain elementary observations on the physical anthropology of race which, though well-known to anatomists, are not, I think, widely enough recognized by those who are concerned with the sociological problems of race. At first sight, the contrast in appearance between such extreme types of mankind as the Negroid, Mongoloid, and

European might suggest fundamental constitutional differences. In fact, however, a close anatomical study seems to show that the physical differences are confined to quite superficial characters. I may best emphasise this by saying that if the body of a Negro were to be deprived of all superficial features such as skin, hair, nose and lips, I do not think that any anatomist could say for certain, in an isolated case, whether he was dealing with the body of a Negro or a European. Naturally, such a test, being limited to the rather crude evidence of gross anatomy, is not by itself to be taken as a final demonstration of the constitutional equivalence of one race with another. Nor does it take account of statistical differences of a relatively minor character. But it does suggest very strongly indeed that the somatic [bodily] differences of race may after all not be of a very fundamental nature. An even more striking fact is that, in spite of statements which have been made to the contrary, there is no macroscopic or microscopic difference by which it is possible for the anatomist to distinguish the brain in single individuals of different races. Now this observation carries with it certain implications which may be of considerable importance, for if we accept the thesis that the brain is the material basis of mental activities, it suggests that the latter are also not fundamentally different in different races."[6]

St. Paul's dictum that "God hath made of one blood all nations of men to dwell on the face of the earth"[7] is in perfect accord with the findings of science.

When, however, scientists speak of the unity of mankind, they do not mean that all men are biologically alike, for obviously they are not; what they mean is that all men are probably derived from a single ancestral stock, for the reasons which have already been adequately given in the passages quoted from Darwin. This is stated in the sentence of the Statement reading *It is further generally agreed among scientists that all men are probably derived from the same common stock*. The striking thing about human beings is their great variability within a common species of fundamental unity; the diversity is comparable to the differences among the members of a single family. The physical differences between the groups of mankind are, in general, more remarkable than those which one sees between the members of a single family. Why?

This question brings us to the next sentence of the Statement, which says that *Such differences as exist between different groups of mankind are due to the operation of evolutionary factors of differentiation such as isolation, the drift and random fixation of the material particles which control heredity (the genes), changes in the structure of these particles, by hybridization, and natural selection.*

These words constitute the briefest statement of the process of evolution with which I am acquainted. It is precise, and I think that any person without specialized knowledge of the subject ought, at least in general terms, have no difficulty in working out for himself what it means. Let us, however, proceed to discuss it in more particular terms.

Isolation and Drift. With the exception of the artificially produced domestic animals, man is possibly among the most variable of mammalian species.[8] Is there, among the mammals, any other single species, always excepting the domesticated animals, which presents such variability in stature, eye color, nose shape, head form, lip form, ear form, body form, and weight, as does man? In what other single species does one find such a variety of types as are represented, for example, by the pygmies, the Hottentots, the Eskimos, and Northwestern European Whites? Whether or not the variability presented by mankind is actually any greater than that exhibited by any other animal species, and at least one authority (Schultz) doubts that it is, the fact remains that that variability is considerable. What does this variability tell us? It tells us that man has almost certainly undergone evolution along the following lines: early differentiation of relatively isolated groups into well-marked geographical races in adaptation to their environment; followed later by intercrossing (hybridization); resulting in an extremely wide range of recombinations of the hereditary particles, the genes.

Let us work all this out step by step. (1) First we start with a single ancestral species population; (2) let us suppose that this population is as variable as are the members of a number of extended families; (3) then let us suppose that a number of individual families at the same and/or at different times migrate away from their tribal center or locality; and (4) that some of the emigrant groups become geographically isolated from each other, and remain so isolated for considerable periods of time.

From the evolutionary standpoint the fundamental materials of evolution are the hereditary particles which are contained in the chromosomes of the sex cells of the male and female members of the population. These hereditary particles, carried in the sex chromosomes, are known as genes. These genes are the units of physiological action which constitute the physical basis of heredity. Among the properties of genes is an inherent capacity to undergo physical change (either in position in relation to other genes or in chemical structure). Such changes in genes or chromosomes are known as mutations. A mutation is a structural change in a gene resulting in a transmissible hereditary modification in the development of a trait. Mutations provide the raw materials of evolution. Without mutation there can be no evolution. A mutant gene exhibits an altered physiological response of the developing organism to the environment, and this may show itself in an alteration of function or structure or both (both are usually involved). A mutation, in interaction with other genes and with the environment, may express itself in such a way as to influence the development of a character in a novel manner.

In each of the isolated groups or populations that we have referred to above, mutations would certainly have occurred independently. Such mutations would probably have affected different genes or different chromosomes, at different times and at different rates, and differently affected different characters. In one geographically isolated group, for example, mutant genes leading to the development of narrow nostrils may have appeared. In another isolated group such mutant genes leading to the development of broad nostrils may have occurred.

If in the environment in which these groups live there is any advantage to the organism in the new form of nostrils, eventually those born with it will have a slight advantage over members of the group who do not possess such nostril form. Individuals with this advantage are likely to leave a greater progeny than those not so endowed, thus, in the course of time, those who are better fitted to their environment are represented in greater number than those who are not. Those who are better adapted to their environments have a differential advantage in reproduction and thus of survival. They are *naturally selected* for survival. Evolution, it has been said, is the sum of adaptation; the maximization of the improbable. Narrow nostrils are, in fact, found most frequently in populations living in cold climates, such as the Eskimos of the Far North, while broad nostrils occur most frequently in populations living in the hot belts of the world. It has been suggested that narrow nostrils allow air to be taken in at a slower rate than broad nostrils and hence afford it an opportunity to be warmed before passing into the lungs.

There is not much doubt that many of man's traits have evolved in this way; that is, by the natural selection of traits which gave their possessors an adaptive advantage which better enabled them to adjust, to adapt to the environment. Not the survival of the fittest, but the survival of the fit.

Almost certainly skin color is such an adaptive trait. We do not yet know why people living in hot climes have dark-pigmented skin, and why those living in cooler climes have lighter pigmented skins. We do know that a dark skin is an effective screen against the harmful ultraviolet rays, and that Whites are more susceptible to skin damage from ultraviolet radiation than Blacks. Obviously, in climates with high sunlight intensity a darkly pigmented skin has a selective advantage in this respect over a white skin.[9]

Differences in body form are also of interest. Populations living in regions of extreme cold, such as those of the Arctic Circle, Siberia, Alaska, and Greenland, tend to be relatively short, and well padded with fat. They present a smaller total surface area of the body than populations long resident in regions of high temperature. The latter would appear to be built to radiate as much heat as possible—the former as little as possible. Flat, padded faces, flattish noses, and "double" upper eyelids—the epicanthic folds of Mongoloid and some other peoples—appear to be adapted to protect the exposed and vulnerable face and eyes from cold.

It is interesting to speculate on the possible reasons for racial differences in hair form, body form, "eye" form, and the like, but at the present time we really don't know the answers and until the necessary researches have been carried out we shall have to wait for the answers.

It is possible that some traits in man have been established in spite of the fact that they have no adaptive value; such traits, for example, as hair form, head shape, and ear size may be of this nature. How would such non-adaptive traits become established in a population? The answer is: by *genetic drift*. Let me explain. In populations which consist of a small number of individuals (and it is believed that most, if not all, early human populations rarely exceeded more than a few hundred individuals) there would be a tendency for purely random accidental fluctuations in the frequencies of certain genes or gene combinations to become fixed in a small inbreeding isolated population. The accidental fluctuation of gene frequencies from generation to generation and their establishment or fixation within a population is known as genetic drift. By this means adaptively neutral or even useless and deleterious changes may be produced in the members of a small population, and by this means alone, isolated populations originally derived from the same ancestral population could come to differ quite substantially from one another. The smaller the size of an isolated population the more likely is genetic drift to be effective. The larger or less isolated a population, the less likely is drift to have any significant effect. Random local differentiation as a result of genetic drift must, then, be taken into consideration as a probable

factor in the differentiation of the races of man. Given
time, isolation, a small population, together with the inherent tendency of the genes to vary, the accidental driftage of genes in this or that unpredictable "direction" is
most likely to occur.

Hybridization or Intercrossing. By hybridization is
meant the crossing of individuals differing from one another in one or more genes or traits.

There are two kinds of hybridization, (1) that achieved
through the sexual process in general which causes recombinations of genes drawn from the common gene pool
of the group, and thus provides the raw material for the
action of natural selection, genetic drift, sexual selection,
and social selection; and (2) intercrossing of distinct populations. Both types of hybridization have played important
roles in the evolution of mankind.

The intercrossing of distinct populations produces a
great increase in the range of recombinations of the hereditary particles, the genes. What we see in the existing
"races" of mankind today would seem to be the effects of
a series of mixtures of "races" which have more or less
settled into states of genetic and physical equilibrium. Intercrossing between populations leads toward the disappearance of "racial" distinctness except in so far as it produces intermediate "racial" groups on geographic boundaries or within a larger population. It is precisely such
intermediate groups which, under conditions of geographic
or social isolation, will develop as so-called geographic
"races."

We are saying, then, that two of the most important
processes in the evolution and diversification of mankind
have been *isolation* and *hybridization followed by isola-*

tion. It is to a very considerable extent through hybridization that the whole great process of change in physical characters (phenotypes = the visible type) occurs. When two populations of somewhat different genetic structure (genotype = genetic type) intercross, there is an exchange of genes to form completely new combinations of genes, and thus a new genotype and a new phenotype.

There is some evidence that the phenomenon of hybrid vigor occurs in man. Hybrid vigor (heterosis) describes the condition in which, as a result of hybridization, the off-spring exceed both parents in size, number of progeny, resistance to disease, and other adaptive qualities. The phenomenon has been observed in the descendants of matings between Polynesians and Englishmen who now live on Pitcairn Island, in the Pacific, for these are said to be of larger size than the average for the members of each of the parental groups. This has also been observed in the offspring of Hottentot-Dutch matings in South Africa. But such changes may have nothing to do with hybrid vigor and may simply reflect the normal effects of mating in man. Upon this subject more research is needed.[10] On the whole we would not expect hybrid vigor to follow "race" mixture, nor would we expect any degeneration or disharmonies in so-called race-crosses, for the simple reason that the gene differences between the races of man are not sufficiently marked. As the distinguished leader of human genetics, Professor L. H. Snyder, has stated, the findings emerging from the study of population genetics lead to the conclusion that human populations differ genetically one from the other almost entirely in the varying *proportions* of the genes of the various sets which they carry and not in the *kinds* of genes they contain.[11] In other words, with the possible exception of a few genes, the differences in the kinds of genes carried by the different "races" of mankind do not appear to be great enough to produce any marked evidences of hybrid vigor. As we shall see, neither are they great enough to produce disharmonies in structure or function.

When it is stated that hybridization or race-crossing is an important factor in producing the diversification of mankind, it should also be obvious that it is one of the most important factors in the unification of mankind, for hybridization always leads to a union of the characters of the hybridizing populations in the resulting hybrid population, and also to increased variation within that population. It is only when a newly formed hybrid group becomes isolated that the new pattern of genes is able to establish itself as in some respects a new population or "race."

Natural Selection. By natural selection is meant the preservation, through the action of the environment, of such variations as arise and are beneficial to the organism under its conditions of life. Because they adapt the organism to those conditions, such variations are called adaptive. Under the selective action of the environment those individuals who possess the necessary adaptive qualities will leave a greater progeny, while those who do not possess the necessary qualities will tend to leave a smaller progeny, and eventually even die out altogether.

Let us quote Darwin's original definition:

"As many more individuals of each species are born than can possibly survive; and as, consequently, there is a frequently recurring struggle for existence, it follows that any being, if it vary however slightly in any manner profitable to itself, under the complex and sometimes varying conditions of life, will have a better chance of surviving, and thus be *naturally selected*. From the strong principle of inheritance, any selected variety will tend to propagate its new and modified form."[12]

It is unnecessary to dwell here any further upon the kind of traits which have probably been naturally selected in the evolution of man in his different racial forms. We have already dealt with such traits above. What I should like to deal with briefly here is the correct way in which natural selection is to be interpreted as acting. In the decades which have elapsed since Darwin's time we have come to understand the nature of natural selection somewhat more clearly. Darwin conceived of natural selection as virtually an exclusively competitive process, and he even went so far as to suggest that in the evolution of man the "struggle" of tribe against tribe in the competition for survival has played an important role, the fittest in the struggle alone surviving. "Extinction," he wrote, "follows chiefly from the competition of tribe with tribe, and race with race."[13] The "extinguishers" in this way proving themselves to be the fittest.

Such evidence as scientists have gathered since Darwin's day lends no support to such a theory either for man or for other animals. Natural selection is a genuine enough process, but it was not altogether accurately interpreted by Darwin. He thought of it largely in terms of "struggle," of "competition," and the "survival of the fittest." The host of interpreters who elaborated Darwin's views and applied them to contemporary societies of man, added further to the fog of misinterpretation. They, like Darwin, asserted that the "inferior races" of man would soon be replaced by the "superior races," since this was an obvious and inescapable law of nature.

The fact is that whatever may be interpreted to occur

in a state of nature among lower animals is not thereby constituted a judgment delivered by "nature" upon man. Altogether apart from the fact that "nature" was fundamentally misinterpreted, the distinguishing trait of man is, among many others, that what is natural to him is to be "unnatural," as it were, to be artificial. Man improves upon nature, he develops a "second nature." He improvises and invents new responses to conditions which other animals may react to, for the most part, somewhat more automatically. His conceptions of what constitutes the good life represent such social inventions. Most men learn these conceptions after they have been established, from the cultures in which they have been raised.[14]

Darwin, T. H. Huxley, and Herbert Spencer realized, but insufficiently stressed, this fact, that the end of the long evolutionary process of man leads not to the survival of the fittest in the struggle for existence, but rather to the survival of the ethically best. Thus, Darwin wrote, "As man advances in civilisation, and small tribes are united into larger communities, the simplest reason would tell each individual that he ought to extend his social instincts and sympathies to all the members of the same nation, though personally unknown to him. This point being once reached, there is only an artificial barrier to prevent his sympathies extending to the men of all nations and races. If, indeed, such men are separated from him by great differences in appearance or habits, experience unfortunately shews us how long it is, before we look at them as our fellow-creatures."[15] The greater part of this passage occurs in the UNESCO Statement on Race, but it cannot be too often repeated as representing the considered viewpoint of a great biologist who is often credited, not altogether unjustly, with holding very contrary views.[16]

Believing that Darwin's interpretation of natural selection was perfectly sound, and accepting it fully, T. H. Huxley, toward the end of his life, was at pains to make it perfectly clear that ". . . the practice of that which is ethically best—what we call goodness or virtue—involves a course of conduct which, in all respects, is opposed to that which leads to success in the cosmic struggle for existence; in place of ruthless self-assertion it demands self-restraint; in place of thrusting aside, or treading down, all competitors, it requires that the individual shall not merely respect, but shall help his fellows; its influence is directed, not so much to the survival of the fittest, as to the fitting of as many as possible to survive. It repudiates the gladiatorial view of existence. . . ." (Huxley had elsewhere earlier written: "from the point of view of the moralist, the animal world is about on the same level as a gladiator's show. The creatures are fairly well treated, and set to fight; whereby the strongest, the swiftest and the cunningest live to fight another day. The spectator has no need to turn his thumb down, as no quarter is given."[17]

Repudiating the "gladiatorial" view of existence, for man at least, Huxley went on to add that "It is from the neglect of these plain considerations that the fanatical individualism of our time attempts to apply the analogy of cosmic nature to society."[18]

So it is clear from these passages that both Darwin and Huxley believed that man's future development lay with the cultivation of his morality, in extending his sympathies, and not merely his respect but also his help, to his fellow man. In these conclusions the whole world of scientists join.

In spite of the recent revival of the view that man is an innately aggressive creature,[19] a view that has been repudiated by most authorities,[20] the fact is that today we know that mutual aid, cooperation, is the dominant principal of life—*not* competition but cooperation—or cooperative competition, for cooperation is the adaptively most successful form of competition. We know that cooperative processes are the basic, though not the only, processes of nature and are characteristic of all living things. It so happens that the biological facts, when properly understood, do give a biological validation to our ethical principles, a biological foundation for our belief in and practice of the Golden Rule: "As ye would that men should do to you, do ye to them likewise." What the Darwinian conception of natural selection lacked was the inclusion of the factor of cooperation. Actually, cooperativeness is an indispensable part, the primary part of the process of evolution. As Professor Paul Burkholder of Yale University has put it, "The most important basis for selection is the ability of associated components to work together harmoniously in the organism and among organisms. All new genetic factors, whether they arise from within by mutation or are incorporated from without by various means, are accepted or rejected according to their cooperation with associated components in the whole aggregation."[21]

The fit are the most cooperative, and those who cooperate best are, in the long run, most likely to survive and leave progeny. Thus, altruism, cooperation, is that form of fitness which is most highly selected for survival in the development of man. This is a fact which cannot be sufficiently underscored. Just as man's physical traits have largely been preserved by natural selection because of their adaptive value, so man in his relations with his fellow man has been preserved and has multiplied because of his ability to adjust himself to what will always remain *the co-*

operative process of living. Selection has favored those who were best able to adapt themselves to their environment.

For man that has meant, among other things, being able to get along with his fellow man, and for societies that has meant being able to get along with other societies of men. Natural selection in human societies is being replaced, so far as man's behavioral development is concerned, by social selection. Through cultural means, by the application of scientific discovery and technical advance, man provides an enormous amount of buffering against the impact of defects which in earlier times would have laid him low, and at the same time provides an enormous variety of niches for virtually every kind of physical and mental type. With the exception of the individual who is in some way totally incapacitated, there increasingly tends to be a place for everyone in such a society. A wide range of niches is available.[22] Cooperation is receiving an increasingly higher reward. The necessity for cooperation in human societies requires no emphasis—without it they would fall apart.[23] Adaptation to the environment is a condition of survival for groups of men either as "races" or societies of whatever kind, as much as it is a condition of survival for groups of organisms. As the noted British archeologist Professor V. Gordon Childe has stated, "the environment to which adaptation is required includes other societies. A device or institution, however well adapted to the needs of a given society and its physical environment, will be permanently beneficial only if it helps that society to adapt itself to its neighbors."[24]

Man's social evolution has been largely a matter of development of those cooperative drives which characterize every living form from the unicellular to the most complex multicellular organism. It should be abundantly clear that in man cooperation must increasingly grow to be the way of life between man and man, and between societies everywhere, if the species is to survive.[25]

The final sentence of Paragraph 1 states that *In these ways* [above described] *groups have arisen of varying stability and degree of differentiation which have been classified in different ways for different purposes.*

This statement is intended to convey the fact that "races" are not fixed, static, or solidified bodies of genes or patterns of traits, but rather that "races" are dynamic systems of biological organizations which are more or less in constant process of change. As Shelley wrote:

Man's yesterday may ne'er be like his morrow;
Naught may endure but mutability.

The rate of visible evolutionary, physical change is relatively slow. We can observe it when looking back from the past to the present, and then only with great difficulty, but we cannot observe it so readily in the present—unless we are fortunate enough to live in such a land as Hawaii. In Hawaii intermarriage between members of the indigenous Polynesian population with Europeans of various national extractions, with Chinese and Japanese, and some other peoples, has resulted in mixtures of genotypes and recombinations of various sorts which afford, indeed, a living example of the kind of thing which must have happened many times in the past history of man.[26] If the present population of Hawaii were isolated from all reproductive contact with members of an outside population there would, in time, undoubtedly appear a new "race" in Hawaii. If there is a "race" in process of formation in Hawaii, it is likely to be in a rather unstable state for many generations, first, because it is in the earliest stages of the process, and second, because it is likely that new gene systems will be more or less constantly introduced by immigrants to disturb whatever approximations to equilibrium the population may be approaching.

"Races" are never static. We see them, superficially, as static only because at our time level they *appear* to be unchanging. But the fact is that all "races" change even in the absence of hybridization. They change, as I have already pointed out, because of the inherent variability of the genes themselves, in addition to the action of other factors. To delimit a "race" is akin to the attempt to freeze a moving stream at a given moment of time.

The degree of differentiation in its physical characters which any "race" has achieved will depend on a number of factors: first, upon the hybridizing elements that have entered into its formation; second, upon the numbers involved in each of the hybridizing groups; third, upon the recency of the crossing and the nature of the physical characters contributed by each group; and fourth, upon the degree of isolation which the group has experienced.

The classification into which such groups have been ordered have differed very widely according to the predilections of the classifier. The number of "races" which different writers have recognized run from as few as three to over one hundred. Some separate their "races" into "pure" and "mixed"; others into "primary," "secondary," and "tertiary." Some classify them by skin color, others by hair form, while others classify them by head shape, and still others by their blood-group gene frequencies. And these are but a few of the systems which have been used.

As a matter of fact, the best we can do at the present

time is to *describe* populations, and while our classifications may be interesting, we must be careful not to take them too seriously. The danger we must avoid is becoming either the caretakers or the captives of our own arbitrary classificatory schemes.

PARAGRAPH 2

From the biological standpoint, the species Homo sapiens is made up of a number of populations, each one of which differs from the others in the frequency of one or more genes. Such genes, responsible for the hereditary differences between men, are always few when compared to the whole genetic constitution of man and to the vast number of genes common to all human beings regardless of the population to which they belong. This means that the likenesses among men are far greater than their differences.

Much that is stated in this paragraph has already been discussed in the analysis of the first paragraph, and will recur again in the discussion of other paragraphs. Therefore let us attempt to clarify for ourselves what this paragraph really means.

First, what do we mean by *the biological standpoint?* We mean from the point of view of the student of life, from the point of view of the zoologist or biologist, who is interested in the evolution and status of man as an animal in the animal kingdom. As such, the biologist finds man to be a typical member of the Class of Mammals, of the Order of Primates (which embraces the lemurlike, monkeylike, and apelike animals), of the Family of Men (Hominidae), of the Genus Man (*Homo*), and the species the wise (*sapiens*), meaning, really, the most highly educable. What is a species? It will be simpler, and the answer will be more easily understood if we ask the question in the plural: What are species? The answer is that species are groups of actually or potentially interbreeding populations, which are reproductively isolated from other such groups. This is the best short definition of species known to me, and it is the definition proposed by Dr. Ernst Mayr of Harvard University.[27] By "reproductively isolated populations" is meant populations of animals which do not and usually cannot breed with other populations of the same genus.

Professor Theodosius Dobzhansky of Rockefeller University defines species as "groups of populations which are reproductively isolated to the extent that the exchange of genes between them is absent or so slow that the genetic differences are not diminished or swamped." By contrast, "Races are defined as populations differing in the incidence of certain genes, but actually exchanging or potentially able to exchange genes across whatever boundaries (usually geographic) separate them."[28]

A species, then, is usually a group of populations. The group is the species, the populations are the "races." The species group as such is reproductively isolated from other related species groups, being either actually unable effectively to breed with, that is to exchange genes with, other similar groups or capable of doing so under conditions which do not affect the specific integrity of the group.

A "race" is one of the group of natural populations comprising the species. The gene differences which distinguish the "racial" groups from one another must be relatively few for the simple reason that all the members of all the different "races" are very much more like than unlike each other. It has been independently estimated that the number of genes which man possesses is perhaps in the vicinity of 30,000.[29] This estimate, arrived at by the use of three different methods, is only an estimate, and no more is claimed for it than that, but it does give us some idea of the number of genes that may be involved in the genetic structure of man. As for the number of gene *differences* which may be involved in any two "races," we can speak only for those few characters for which we understand the genetic mechanism, and speculate about the remainder. Upon this basis all competent students who have considered the subject believe that by far the greatest number of genes are held by mankind in common, and that there are propably not more than 10 per cent of the total that are held apart.[30] Since scientists believe that mankind drew its genes originally from the same gene pool, this great likeness is not surprising.

As soon as we get beneath the skin, the likeness on a physical basis would suggest that the number of gene differences existing between even the most "extreme" "races" of man is much less than 10 per cent. I have already quoted Professor Le Gros Clark in this connection.

It is important to emphasize in one's own mind and to grasp the significance of this substantive likeness of all the varieties of mankind.

> Where order in variety, we see
> And where, tho' all things differ, all agree.
>
> *Pope*

The theory has been proposed by Professor Carleton S. Coon that modern man, *Homo sapiens,* evolved from the single species *Homo erectus,* not once but five times. The five different subspecies, each evolving independently and arriving at the *sapiens* state at different times, "each had followed a pathway of its own through the labyrinth of time. Each had been molded in a different fashion to meet the needs of different environments, and each had reached its own level on the evolutionary scale."[31]

The probabilities are that had the presumed subspecies

of man developed in the kind of independent isolation Coon postulates they would, owing to the inherent variability of the genetic constitution, have come to exhibit, among other things, far greater differences in their structures and appearance in their earlier and more recent forms than they, in fact, do.

Coon believes that the Negroids were the last of the subspecies of *Homo erectus* to be transformed into *sapiens.* Hence, since the Negroids do not have as long a history as *sapiens* as do the Caucasoids, "it is a fair inference that fossil men now extinct were less gifted than their descendants who have larger brains, that the subspecies which crossed the evolutionary threshold into the category of *Homo sapiens* the earliest have evolved the most, and that the obvious correlation between the length of time a subspecies has been in the *sapiens* state and the levels of civilization attained by some of its populations may be related phenomena."

According to Professor Coon, "As far as we know now," the African Negro line "started on the same evolutionary level as the Eurasiatic ones in the Early Middle Pleistocene and then stood still for half a million years, after which Negroes and Pygmies appeared as if out of nowhere." The catch here lies in the "As far as we know now." And what we in fact know now is precisely so unilluminatingly little relating to the physical evolution of Negroes, that the half million years of standing still, which the Negroes supposedly did, represents nothing more nor less than a lacuna in our knowledge concerning the Negro's physical evolution. Even the surface of the subject has not yet been scratched, for the materials which would enable us to reconstruct the barest outline of Negro evolution are simply not available.

Professor Coon's views give great comfort to racists, but they find no support among scientists.

The biological facts provide the proof of the unity of man, and at the same time, provide a biological foundation for the social unity of mankind. Members of different races resemble each other far more closely than they differ from each other. Such differences as exist between them are few and, for the most part, superficial. Few and superficial as most of them are, it would be foolish to attempt to minimize them out of existence, if not as unfortunate as the attempt to exaggerate the importance of these differences. The history of our fellow men and of ourselves in relation to them ought never to cease to interest us. Points of difference ought to be matters of interest and wonder to us. It should be exciting and enlarging to learn how our fellow men and ourselves, in all our variety, got to be the way we are. This is one of the objects of the science of anthropology, the science of man.[32]

PARAGRAPH 3

A race, from the biological standpoint, may therefore be defined as one of the group of populations constituting the species Homo sapiens. These populations are capable of interbreeding with one another but, by virtue of the isolating barriers which in the past kept them more or less separated, exhibit certain physical differences as a result of their somewhat different biological histories. These represent variations, as it were, on a common theme.

This paragraph largely repeats what is expressed in other words in Paragraph 2, and has been elaborated in the discussions of both Paragraphs 1 and 2. It states more simply and sharply, in common language, what, from the biological standpoint, a "race" is.

Reference has already been made to the *different biological histories* which the different races of man have experienced. They have been traced from an original common ancestry, through separation and isolation from the ancestral stock; spontaneous change in some genes (mutation); the action of natural selection upon those traits in the individual and in the group, which better adapt them to their environment; the action of genetic drift or the random driftage of genes and their fixation in determinate patterns for traits which are adaptively neutral; hybridization; and the like.

Two factors which may have played a significant role in the differentiation of the "races" of man are *sexual selection* and *social selection*.

Ever since Darwin first developed the conception in

The Descent of Man (1871), sexual selection has come to mean the selection by the best equipped males of the most preferred females. The best endowed males, according to Darwin, tend to crowd out the less well-endowed males in the matter of reproduction. The traits of the latter are thus less likely to be perpetuated through sexual selection. The traits thus selected by the successful males are likely, in the course of time, to bring about modifications in the females, and by this means, eventually, in the whole population. Functionally, sexual selection could be defined as the process of selecting mates on the basis of a preferred standard of beauty or other desirable quality, so that in the course of time the sexually preferred type would become the dominant one in the group, and perhaps cause the non-preferred type to become a separate isolate, or even die out.

For example, in a group in which "frizzly" hair was preferred to straight hair, the straight-haired individuals would find fewer and fewer mates and thus increasingly leave a smaller progeny behind them, until the genes for straight hair ceased to exist altogether, or the frizzly-haired would mate with the frizzly-haired, and the straight-haired with straight-haired, and thus two distinct types would be formed. The preference of dark Black males for lighter-skinned Black females in America constitutes an example of the manner in which sexual selection operates to reduce the darkness of the Black skin.[33] The preference of brunets for blonds is an illustration of how sexual selection serves to maintain a balanced distribution of such types. Since the differentiation of human groups could, at least in part, be brought about through the sexual selection of traits possessing no adaptive value other than in relation to some arbitrary standard of beauty, sexual selection is a possible factor to be considered in the discussion of the manner in which human "races" came to be differentiated.

It is, however, difficult to evaluate the role which sexual selection may have played in the early differentiation of human "races." Darwin thought that role a considerable one. Today we cannot be so sure. When we turn to existing nonliterate societies at the technologically most undeveloped levels for enlightenment[34] upon this point we find that in such societies almost everyone marries, and there is little or no evidence of sexual selection. It is unlikely that conditions were otherwise in early human populations, and a doubt may legitimately be expressed as to the importance of sexual selection in man's early history. In more highly developed nonliterate societies sexual selection *is* a factor of some importance. In the recent period of man's history, there can be no doubt that sexual selection has to an increasing extent been operative, nor can there be any doubt that it will continue to be so in the future.

By *social selection* is meant the regulation of breeding by artificially instituted barriers between socially differentiated individuals or groups within a population, so that mating occurs between individuals preferred by such social standards, rather than at random. Under such conditions strong isolating mechanisms are developed which, in the course of time, may produce considerable modifications in a population. Where, for example, as in America, there are a variety of colored populations, "Black," "Brown," and "Yellow," social barriers more or less effectively tend to keep these groups separate from one another and from the White population. In this way such barriers act as isolating mechanisms akin to natural physiographic isolating factors, which have a similar effect in maintaining the genetic differences between isolated groups.

Let us consider the manner in which social selection acts upon the structure of the population of the United States. Until recently intermarriage between Blacks and Whites was forbidden by some 32 states of the Union[35]; in the remainder it is still socially strongly discouraged. Now, while social barriers effectively limit the Blacks biological participation in the reproductive structure of the White population, nevertheless a relatively small number of individuals of Negroid ancestry are continually trickling into the ranks of the White population.[36] This trickle is largely a consequence of the more or less limited effectiveness of the social barriers and the asymmetric sexual relations which prevail between the two groups, the only relationship (covertly) tolerated being between White men and Black women. In the North marriages between Black males and White females have been, and remain, too few to make any significant difference to the genetic structure of the population as a whole. What happens as a result of this socially regulated mixture is that (1) the Black population loses a certain number of its descendants by their "passing" into the White population, (2) but it gains a proportion of "White" genes. Thus, by the first means a small proportion of "Black" genes pass into the White population, and by the second means a larger proportion of "White" genes pass into the Black population. The White population being more than ten times as large as the Black population, the small proportion of "Black" genes passing into it are rapidly absorbed and scattered, and have no recognizable effect upon the White population as a whole. On the other hand the flow of "White" genes into the Black population has apparently been quite considerable, for the effects of those genes are obvious to everyone who has lived in the United States.[37] It is considered by most authorities that over 70 per cent of American Blacks are of mixed Black-White ancestry, with the Black ancestors predominating. Of this 70 per cent a large proportion shows the evidences of intermixture in its physical characters, for instance, in the longer, narrower nose, lighter skin, thinner lips, larger ears, less frizzly hair, and so on.[38]

What we observe, then, is that the physical character of the Black population is being changed by the introduction into it, from the larger White group, of genes which tend to approximate the Black population toward the white. If this process goes on at the same rate at which it is now proceeding, no significant changes in the changing pattern of Black traits is likely to occur; but if the process is accelerated—as it will almost certainly be—then it is probable that the Black group will, in time, become a distinctive "racial" group in itself, a "racial" group differing from any other known "racial" group. And this new American Black "race" will have been produced largely through the action of a socially regulated process of hybridization. Some anthropologists believe that the American Black already exhibits distinctive physical norms.[39]

PARAGRAPH 4

*I*n short, the term "race" designates a group or population characterized by some concentrations, relative as to frequency and distribution, of hereditary particles (genes) or physical characters, which appear, fluctuate, and often disappear in the course of time by reason of geographic and/or cultural isolation. The varying manifestations of these traits in different populations are perceived in different ways by each group. What is perceived is largely preconceived, so that each group arbitrarily tends to misinterpret the variability which occurs as a fundamental difference which separates that group from all others.

The statements in this paragraph attempt to underscore the fact that all racial groups constitute but temporary structures, as it were, which genetically are made up of temporary mixtures of genes derived from a mixed ancestry. The stability which any "race" may exhibit in its physical traits, and the equilibrium[40] which it may exhibit in its genetic structure, is always only apparent, for changes are constantly proceeding in the genetic structure of all "races," even though it may take a long time for those changes to become visible. All "races" are at best but temporarily stable because (1) mutations are constantly accumulating within the population and eventually exert their cumulative effect, (2) genetic drift by the fixation of random variations in gene frequencies and the extinction of some genes, alters its character, and (3) hybridization at one time or another is the inevitable lot of most "races." It is for these reasons that we may correctly think of human "races" as representing *temporary* concentrations of genetic systems. "Temporary" means lasting only for a time. So far as "lasting" or stability of human "races" are concerned, if a racial group is isolated for an appreciable period of time, there will be a scattering of genes throughout the population so that every generation will exhibit the same genetic structure or genotype with the same frequencies, in respect to particular genes or arrangements of genes. Such a population is said to be in *genetic equilibrium*. Such a population may endure relatively unchanged for a very long time as long as it remains isolated, although, as I have already pointed out, small changes will occur within it continuously. Hence, while emphasizing the instability of "races," let us also emphasize the fact that "races" are also capable of a certain very real stability, even though it is always a temporary stability. The fact, however, which it is most important to remember is that a "race" is not something fixed, permanent, and unchanging or unchangeable, but that it is a dynamic, potentially unstable entity, which is seen to be stable only when one delimits the process of change at one's own time level. Seen at another time, at another period, in another century, another millennium, it may be a very different "race," depending upon the kind of influences which have been operative upon it during the interval of elapsed time.[41]

Thus genes may be altered in the frequency distribution with which they occur in a "race;" the genes may actually fluctuate in their frequencies for a time and eventually some of them may become extinct. This, quite probably, has happened to blood group B among certain American Indians. Among certain groups of the Navaho Indians of the Southwest, the gene for blood group B has been wholly or almost wholly extinguished. In some Asiatic Mongoloid people the rare Rh^z gene is present in rather low frequencies. These frequencies could be changed in a relatively short time through the operation of such factors as we have already discussed. Geographic

or cultural isolation, that is, social isolation of one group
by another within the same society (social selection) are
two factors which are specially mentioned in this connection.

In looking at the "races" of mankind today, what we
see are largely the stages of development which they are in
at our particular time. The varying manifestations of
physical traits which they exhibit are not "end-results" but
bills of exchange, as it were, drawn on the bank of time,
negotiable securities which can be turned into the coin of
any realm with which it is sought to have biological relations. In other words, we perceive the consequences of
different histories of biological experience in the "races"
of today. Unfortunately, what we see, what we per-ceive
(*per* = by, through, *capere* = to take), is largely based on
the kingdom that is within us. What we do with the objects of the outside world is to take them in and pass them
through all that our experience, biological and social, has
made us—the alembic of ourselves—and then judge them
according to that experience. In short, our perceptions
come not from the objects we judge, but from ourselves,
and what we judge things to be depends not so much upon
the things as upon what we ourselves are in terms of the
history of our own past experience.[42] That is why it is said
that what we perceive is preconceived, for a perception is
not a new sensation, a mere appearance reflecting reality,
but it is a sensation which has been invested with *meaning*, a meaning entirely determined by our past experience. As that experience has been, so will we judge. We
judge according to experience, *not* according to reality,
and for most of us experience conditions what we take to
be reality.

Not understanding the nature of the differences involved, the members of populations that are addicted to

exaggerating the importance of certain kinds of differences will easily be led by their social conditioning to perceive major differences where there are only minor ones, inferiority where in fact only differences exist, and fundamental differences where the differences are in reality only superficial. For that is what the differences between the races of mankind are: superficial, skin-deep. No matter how far we may want, as scientists, to lean over backwards and say, "Do not let us minimize the interesting differences which exist in the physical traits of mankind," the fact is that at their most marked, as in the "peppercorn" hair of Bushmen and the straight hair of Whites, to take two of the most extreme differences, the resemblance between them still remains greater than the resemblance between the straight hair of an ape and the straight hair of a White man.

The differences, by whatever scientific scale we wish to evaluate them, remain interesting, and whether by any such scale we call them "large" or "small," "major" or "minor," is a purely arbitrary matter, so long as we are not led to exaggerate the importance of the differences, for to do so is always to misinterpret their significance. When differences are exaggerated, likenesses are obscured. As the Statement puts it in Paragraph 2, "The likenesses among men are far greater than their differences." Properly understood and evaluated, the differences between the "races" of men become matters of interest and lead to admiration—for what can be more interesting than the history of ourselves in all the varying manifestations in which we are displayed as members of "racial" groups; and what, in these matters, is worthy of greater wonder and admiration than the variety of adaptations with which mankind has responded to the varying demands which have been made upon it by its varying environments?

PARAGRAPH 5

These are the scientific facts. Unfortunately, however, when most people use the term "race" they do not do so in the sense above defined. To most people, a race is any group of people whom they choose to describe as a race. Thus, many national, religious, geographic, linguistic or cultural groups have, in such loose usage, been called a "race," when obviously Americans are not a race, nor are Englishmen, nor Frenchmen, nor any other national group. Catholics, Protestants, Moslems, and Jews are not races, nor are groups who speak English or any other language thereby definable as a race; people who live in Iceland or England or India are not races, nor are people who are culturally Turkish or Chinese or the like thereby describable as races.

The term "race," as used in popular parlance, is perhaps the most confused and most confusing term in the language. One finds people speaking of the "French race," "the German race," "the Moslem and Jewish races," "the Indian race," "the Aryan race," and so on.

The French and German peoples are no more races than is the American people. The French, Germans, and American peoples are nations, *not* races. They in no way correspond to the description of races which we have already given. A nation is a people living under the same government and inhabiting the same country. A nation may be, and frequently is, made up of a number of different mixed "racial" groups. The United States of America, for instance, is "one nation indivisible," which is made up of members of some of the following "races," Whites of all European nations, African Negroes mainly from West Africa, Mongoloids from Japan and China and the indigenous North American Indians, Puerto Ricans, Filipinos, and Eskimos, while Hawaiians contribute Polynesian elements whether or not they are already mixed with Europeans and Mongoloids. Obviously, a people constituted of different "races" which, to a large extent, retain something of their "racial" distinctness, cannot be called a "race." There is no such thing as an American "race." There is such a thing as an American nation. It is incorrect to speak of the first, and correct to speak of the second.

I have chosen the American nation to illustrate what has been true of so many other nations because America shows this so much better than these others; namely, the diversity of "racial" elements which have entered into the formation of every nation. The history of the American nation is so much more recent than any of the other nations of the world, and its history is so clear, that we see distinctly what in the course of time has been blurred in the case of so many other nations. The confusion between "nations" and "race" is more understandable than the confusion between religion and "race." One never hears anyone speak of the Protestant or of the Catholic race. It may be supposed that this is because most people are familiar with the fact that both Whites and Blacks, for example, can be members of the same religion. The religions with which most people in the United States are familiar are the Protestant and the Catholic. The less familiar religions such as the Moslem and the Jewish are likely to provide a handle by which to misname their adherents. Thus, at one time, they may be referred to as members of the "Moslem nation" and at another as members of the "Moslem race." *"The"* Jews are perhaps the most sinned against people in this respect. I emphasize the article because one always refers to *the* Jews, while, in general, references to peoples of other religions will be made without the article. One doesn't speak of *"the* Catholics" or *"the* Protestants," but simply of "Catholics" and

"Protestants." Not that it is incorrect to speak of *"the* Jews," because as it so happens, and as most people have realized, *"the"* Jews are something in addition to being members of the Jewish religion. Where the error is made is to identify this "something" with a particular "race," and to call such people members of the Jewish "race."

The fact is that there is not now nor was there ever a Jewish race. There are such things as a Jewish religion and a Jewish culture; and furthermore many Jews exhibit the evidences of an ancestry derived from populations similar to those living in the Near East at the present time. There are three different conditions, then, which generally serve to distinguish many members of the Jewish faith from the majority of other persons within the population of which they form a part. These are religion, cultural differences, that is to say differences in the way of life and in behavior, and in a certain proportion, physical traits which differ sufficiently from those of the rest of the population to make them readily identifiable. The combination of these conditions in many Jews makes it possible to recognize them as such.

It should be clear that any person who subscribes to the tenets of the Jewish religion and practices them is a Jew by religion. That fact, however, tells us nothing about his "race." There are Mongoloid Chinese who are Jews, Abyssinian and American Blacks who are Jews, and in Italy there is a whole village of ex-Catholic Mediterraneans who are Jews. These are all members of different "racial" stocks. Obviously, then, the Jewish religion is not a mark of any "race" whatsoever since any member of any "race" may belong to it. As for people who are identified with "the" Jews, they are drawn from probably more heterogeneous sources than any other identifiable people in

the world. The ethnic ingredients entering into the formation of the group called Jews have not undergone mixture in a common melting pot, but remain very various.
Clearly, then, the Jews are not anything approaching a
homogeneous, biological entity, nor are they a "race" or
an ethnic group. Many Jews from all over the world have
recently joined in forming the Israeli nation, but neither
"race" nor religion is identifiable with the Israeli nation,
for there are numerous Israelis who are not Jews by religion, and are certainly not Jews by any biological or
"racial" standard. A member of the Israeli nation should,
therefore, be called an "Israeli" and not a "Jew." Strictly
speaking, a person is a Jew only when he is a practicing
member of the Jewish faith. However, it is a fact that
many persons who have either given up their Jewish religion or let it go by default, and still others who were
brought up in homes in which there had been no religious
teaching, are nevertheless identifiable as Jews. What is the
explanation for this if it is not "race"?

There are several explanations which may be operative.
In the first place, a proportion of Jews retains an aggregation of Mediterranean physical traits. In any population not exhibiting such an aggregation of physical traits,
some persons would be easily recognizable as Jews by virtue of this difference. But this is not to say that such
physical traits are peculiar to all or most Jews, for, in fact,
a large proportion of Jews do not possess such traits.[43]
Nor does it mean that some Jews alone possess the aggre-
gate of physical traits referred to, for many of the non-
Jewish populations of the Near and Middle East as well
as of the Mediterranean exhibit such traits in much
higher frequencies than do "the" Jews.

In the second place, some Jews possess a certain quality

of looking "Jewish," but again this quality is not peculiar to Jews alone, for it is the "look" which characterizes most of the peoples of the Near and Middle East. In the Occident persons of such origins are frequently taken for Jews. This "Jewish-looking" quality, occurring in any population not generally characterized by it, renders it possible to recognize some persons as being Jews. Even so, one will often go wrong and mistakenly identify as Jews persons of no Jewish affiliation whatever, such as many Italians, Greeks, Turks, Arabs, Berbers, and related peoples. The quality of looking Jewish is therefore associated with a certain physical type, the Mediterranean type, but it is a type to which only some persons of Jewish faith or culture conform, while it is characteristic of a vastly greater number of people who are not Jews.

A third means by which a certain proportion of persons of Jewish affiliation may be distinguished is the cultural, that is to say, the general way in which persons behave. There is such a thing as a Jewish culture. Any person who has been brought up, conditioned in a Jewish cultural environment, is likely to acquire a personality structure which is unique to such persons, as is the uniqueness of the personality structure of any person acquired in any other particular culture. Such traits are cultural traits, *not* biological ones. They make those who have been differently culturalized socially "visible" to each other. In the case of Jews, such cultural traits, taken collectively, differ sufficiently from those which prevail in the communities in which Jews generally live, to render many of them distinguishable from most of the other members of these communities. But this kind of visibility, it must again be emphasized, is cultural in essence and *not* biological, although the physical appearance of the individual may add to the confused notion that the traits which render it possible to identify a person as a Jew constitutes a proof of the reality of such a thing as a Jewish "race." In fact, as I hope I have shown, there is no such thing as a Jewish "race." It is one of the world's great illusions.[44]

The nearest approximation to a group identification for "the" Jew would be as a tribe.[45] It should be obvious that by virtue of the fact that people live in a particular geographic area or region they are not thereby converted into a race. Some races do occupy specific territories to which they are restricted, such as the Andaman Islanders, the Congo pygmies, the Australian aborigines, and others, but there are also other peoples living in these areas, and the fact that the former and the latter live in definite territories thereby makes none of them a "race." Geographic isolating factors have, as we have seen, a great deal to do with the formation of races, but that is quite another thing from saying that geographic habitat is equivalent to or determines "race." Americans are not a "race" because they live in America, nor are the Germans a "race" because they live in the circumscribed region of Europe known as Germany; the people who inhabit Tasmania are not a "race" because they live in Tasmania—as a matter of fact, the vast majority of them are of European origin. Race cuts across geographic boundaries. The people of such lands as Iceland, England, and India are not "races." The first two are Whites of Northwestern European type, like millions of other whites distributed all over the world, while India is made up of no one yet knows how many different "racial" groups some of whom are scarcely distinguishable, say, from the people of Tibet and Ceylon.

The identification of "race" with language has been frequently and erroneously made. Obviously, not all people who speak English are members of a non-existent English "race." The same is clearly true of all European languages, and of the languages of many nonliterate peoples. For example, some 140 different languages were spoken by the Indians of North America. Most tribes had their own language or dialect, but this does not mean that the population of North America was made up of 140 different "races." It is doubtful whether the pre-Columbian population of North American Indians was made up of as many as six "races." Some languages, among nonliterate peoples, are peculiar to the particular "race," as among the Andaman Islanders, but these are the exceptions rather than the rule.

Finally, it should be clear that culture, the way of life of a people, is not determined by "race" and that "race" is not determined by culture. The culture of America is the culture of a people constituted of several "races," "White," "Black," "Red," and "Yellow." And clearly the culture of America is largely derived from Europe, and hence from many different European ethnic groups. The culture of an Australian aboriginal tribe is not the culture of the whole Australian "race" or the two or three "races" of which it has recently been said to be comprised. Whether there be one or more Australian aboriginal "races," these are split up into many different tribes, most of them with their own distinctive culture. The same was true for American Indians—one or more "races" with many tribes, most of them with their own distinctive culture.

PARAGRAPH 6

National, religious, geographic, linguistic, and cultural
  groups do not necessarily coincide with racial
groups; and the cultural traits of such groups have no
demonstrated genetic connection with racial traits. Because serious errors of this kind are habitually committed where the term "race" is used in popular parlance,
it would be better when speaking of human races to drop
the term "race" altogether and speak of ethnic groups.

I t is clear, then, that national, religious, geographic, linguistic, and cultural groups do not necessarily coincide with "racial" groups. The declaration that *the cultural traits of such groups have no demonstrated genetic
connection with racial traits* will be dealt with in the discussion of Paragraph 10. Let us, therefore, deal here with
the suggestion that because serious errors of the kind already discussed are habitually committed when the term
"race" is used in popular parlance, it would be better
when speaking of human races to drop the term "race" altogether and speak of *ethnic groups*.

Note that the reference is to "popular parlance." It is
not recommended that scientists and those who know
what they are talking about drop the term "race." We
have already defined "race" in the sense in which it may
justly and scientifically be used. But it *is* recommended
that even scientists and other knowledgeable persons
when, in non-scientific circles, refer to any more or less
delimitable human group which *may* represent a "racial"
group or be akin to one, use the term *ethnic group* instead
of "race."

The value of this procedure lies in the fact that it is easier to re-educate people by introducing a new conception with a new term, particularly when it is desired to remove a prevailing erroneous conception and substitute a new and more accurate one. The greatest obstacle to the process of re-education would be the retention of the old term "race," which enshrines so many of the errors which it is desirable to remove. Another advantage of the term *ethnic group* is that it is noncommittal. One may use it as equivalent to the definition of race in the biological sense, but one can use it also of groups which are less clearly defined, which may or may not be races and hence which should not be called races in the absence of the necessary scientific demonstration. All that we say when we use the term *ethnic group* is that here is a group of people who physically, and perhaps in other ways, may be regarded as a more or less distinct group. Until we know what they really are, and until we understand thoroughly what we are talking about with respect to this and all other groups, let us call all such groups *ethnic groups*. In other words, the concept of *ethnic group* implies a question mark, *not* a period. It implies that many questions remain to be asked, and that many answers will have to be given before we can say what precisely any particular *ethnic* group represents.[46]

Furthermore, the very usage of the phrase *ethnic group* has considerable re-educative value. Each time it is used it is likely to elicit the question, "What do you mean by *ethnic group*?" Whereas, every time one uses the term "race," everyone, of course, thinks he knows what *that* means, when the chances are that what he understands by "race" is largely false. The term *ethnic group* thus gives every user an opportunity to participate in the process of re-education as well as of self-enlightenment. When the word "race" is uttered it usually evokes a stereotyped series of prejudices which almost everyone takes for granted as the meaning of a fact requiring no further explanation. On the other hand the term *ethnic group* stimulates inquiry and a new trend of thought. In short, the term *ethnic group* serves as a challenge to thought and as a stimulus to rethink the foundations of one's beliefs. For the layman the term "race" closes the door on his understanding; the term *ethnic group* opens it.[47]

It might be argued that since races in various biological senses of the word can be conceived to exist in man, it would seem unnecessary to drop this long-established term in favor of some other. The truth, however, is that there are so many different senses in which even biologists use the term, that many leading members of that profession prefer not to use it at all. Huxley, a biologist, and Haddon, a physical anthropologist, repudiated the term in 1936.[48] Calman recommended that the term "variety" should be avoided altogether and suggested that "Other terms such as 'geographical race,' 'form,' 'phase,' and so forth, may be useful in particular instances but are better not used until some measure of agreement is reached as to their precise meaning."[49] Kalmus writes: "A very important term which was originally used in systematics is 'race.' Nowadays, however, its use is avoided as far as possible in genetics."[50] In a more recent work Kalmus writes, "It is customary to discuss the local varieties of humanity in terms of 'race.' However, it is unnecessary to use this greatly debased word, since it is easy to describe populations without it."[51] G. S. Carter, in his book on *Animal Evolution,* writes that the terms "'race,' 'variety,' and 'form' are used so loosely and in so many senses that it is advisable to avoid using them as infraspecific categories."[52] Professor Ernst Hanhart denies that there are any "true races" in man,[53] and Professor L. S. Penrose, in a review of Dunn and Dobzhansky's little book *Heredity, Race and Society,* writes that he is unable to "see the necessity for the rather apologetic retention of the obsolete term 'race,' when what is meant is simply a given population differentiated by some social, geographical or genetical character, or . . . merely by a gene frequency peculiarity. The use of the almost mystical concept of race makes the presentation of the facts about the geographical and linguistic groups . . . unnecessarily complicated."[54] In commenting on the subject J. P. Garlick has remarked that "The use of 'race' as a taxonomic unit for man seems out-of-date if not irrational."[55]

In spite of these strictures many biologists will continue to use the term, and if they can use it in an adequately defined manner so that their meaning can be clearly understood by other scientists, erroneous though that usage may be, it will be all the more easy for the critic to direct attention to the sources of the error. It cannot be too frequently emphasized that definitions are not to be achieved at the beginning of an inquiry but only at the end of one. Such inquiries have not yet been completed to the satisfaction of most scientists who have paid considered attention to the subject of "race." The term, therefore, at best is at the present time not really allowable on any score in man. One may or may not be of the opinion that the term "race" ought to be dropped altogether from the vocabulary, because it is so prematurely defined and confusing and because biologists and other scientists are frequently guilty of using it incorrectly, and that therefore it would be better if they did not lend the aura of their authority to the use of so confusing a word. The term "subspecies" has been used as the equivalent of the term "race," but this suffers from the same disadvantages, and has been as misused as its equivalent.[56] The term "race" is so embarrassed by confused and mystical meanings, and has so many blots upon its escutcheon, that a discouragement of its use would constitute an encouragement to clearer thinking.

In opposition to this view a number of objections have been expressed. One doesn't change anything by changing names. It's an artful dodge. Why not meet the problem head-on? If, in popular usage, the term "race" has been befogged and befouled, why not cleanse it of the smog and foulness and restore it to its pristine condition? Re-education should be attempted by establishing the true meaning of "race," not by denying its existence. One cannot combat racism by enclosing the word in quotes. It is not the word that requires changing but people's ideas about it. It is a common failing to argue from the abuse of an idea to its total exclusion. And so on.

It was Francis Bacon who remarked that truth grows more readily out of error than it does out of confusion. The time may come when it may be possible for most men to use the term "race" in a legitimate scientific sense, with clarity and with reason. But that time is not yet. It does not appear to be generally realized that while stone walls do not a prison make, scientific terms are capable of doing so. Until people are soundly educated to understand the muddlement of ideas which is represented by such terms as "race" they will continue to believe in absurdities. And as Voltaire so acutely remarked, "As long as people believe in absurdities they will continue to commit atrocities." Words are what men breathe into them. Men have a strong tendency to use words and phrases which cloak the unknown in the undefined or undefinable. As Housman put it, "calling in ambiguity of language to promote confusion of thought."[57]

The layman's conception of "race" is so confused and emotionally muddled that any attempt to modify it would seem to be met by the greatest obstacle of all, the term "race" itself. This is another reason why the attempt to retain the term "race" in popular parlance must fail. The term is a trigger word; utter it and a whole series of emotionally conditioned responses follow. The phrase *ethnic group* suffers from no such defect. If we are to clarify the minds of those who think in terms of "race" we must cease using the word primarily because in the layman's mind the term defines conditions which do not in fact exist. There is no such thing as the kind of "race" in which the layman believes. If we are to re-educate him in a sound conception of the meaning of that population or somatological or genetic group which we prefer to designate by the general and non-committal phrase *ethnic group,* then it would seem far more reasonable to convey to him the temporariness of the situation with a general rather than with a particular term. This is particularly desirable when it is sought to remove a prevailing erroneous conception and substitute one that clarifies without solidifying. Professor Henry Sigerist has well said that "it is never sound to continue the use of terminology with which the minds of million of people have been poisoned even when the old terms are given new meanings."[58] And Professor George Gaylord Simpson has written, "A word for which everyone has a different definition, usually unstated, ceases to serve the function of communication and its use results in futile arguments about nothing. There is also a sort of Gresham's Law for words; redefine them as we will, their worst or most extreme meaning is almost certain to remain current and to tend to drive out the meaning we might prefer."[59] Bertrand Russell has suggested that for words that have strong emotional overtones we should substitute in our arguments the letters of the alphabet.

The biologist who has been largely concerned with the study of animal populations will be likely to take an oversimplified view of the problems here involved and to dismiss such attempts at re-education of the layman as unsatisfactory. By substituting one term for another, he will say, one solves nothing. It is quite as possible to feel "ethnic group prejudice" as it is to feel "race prejudice." Perhaps. But this kind of comment indicates that the real point has been missed. The phrase *ethnic group* is *not* a substitute for the term "race." The grounds upon which it is suggested constitute a fundamental difference in viewpoint which significantly differentiates what the phrase stands for from what the term stands for. It is not a question of changing names, and there is no question of resorting to devices or artful dodges—the imputation would be silly. If what the phrase *ethnic group* means is clearly understood and accepted, "ethnic group prejudice" would hardly require to be taken seriously. There have been some who have felt that the use of the phrase *ethnic group* was an avoidance of the main issue. On the other hand, most students of human nature would take the view that such a usage constitutes a more realistic and more promising approach to the problem of lay thinking on this subject than the method of attempting to put new meaning into the old bottle of "race." I agree with Korzybski that "because of the great semantic influence of the structure of language on the masses of mankind, leading, as it does, through lack of better understanding and *evaluation* to *speculation on terms,* it seems advisable to abandon completely terms which imply to the *many* the suggested elementalism, although these terms are used in a proper non-elementalistic way by the few."[60]

The ground on which the phrase *ethnic group* is principally suggested is that it is easier to re-educate people by introducing a new conception with a new distinctive term, particularly, I repeat, when it is desired to remove a prevailing erroneous conception and introduce a new and more accurate one. Those who do not understand that the greatest obstacle to the process of re-education would be the retention of the old term "race," a term which enshrines the errors it is desired to remove, do not understand the deep implicit meanings which this word has inescapably come to possess for so many of its users. This question may, then, be asked: Will the phrase *ethnic group* be sufficient to cause such persons to alter their ideas? The answer is for some "No," for others, "It will help"; and for still others, "Yes." No one should be so naïve as to suppose that by this means alone one is going to solve the "race" problem! The suggestions here made are calculated to help; they can do no more at best. Each time one uses the term "race" most individuals believe they understand what is meant, when in fact the chances are that what they understand by the term is largely false. "Race" is something so familiar that in speaking of it one takes one's private meaning completely for granted and one never thinks to question it. On the other hand, when one uses the phrase *ethnic group* wherever "race" would have been used, the question is generally asked: "What do you mean by *ethnic group?*" And that at once affords the opportunity to discuss the facts and explain their meaning as well as the falsities of the prevailing conception of "race." This, it seems to me, is one of the greatest educational advantages of the phrase *ethnic group* over the term "race." Another advantage of the phrase is that it leaves all question of definition open, it refers specifically to human populations which are believed to exhibit a certain degree, amount, or frequency of undetermined physical likenesses or homogeneity. An ethnic group has already been described as one of a number of populations, which populations together comprise the species *Homo sapiens,* and which individually maintain their differences, physical and cultural, by means of isolating mechanisms such as geographic and social barriers. These differences vary as the power of the geographic and social barriers vary. Where these barriers are of high power, such ethnic groups will tend to remain distinct from each other geographically or ecologically.

By a "population" is meant a Mendelian population, that is an intrabreeding group. By the random interchange of genes within such groups and other genetic processes, a certain commonality of traits is often established and maintained within such populations. The processes of evolution and differentiation of such natural groups is a principal concern of the physical anthropologist. English and English write as follows, "Ethnic group is an intentionally vague or general term used to avoid some of the difficulties of *race.* The ethnic group may be a nation, a people (such as the Jews), a language group (the Dakota Indians), a sociologically defined so-called race (the American Negro), or a group bound together in a coherent cultural entity by a religion (the Amish)."[61] To which one may add that the group may be characterized by a certain unity of genetic or physical traits.

Yet another advantage of the phrase *ethnic group* is that it avoids the reductionist or "nothing but" fallacy, that is to say, the notion that men are nothing but the resultant of their biological heredity, that they are what they are because of their genes. The phrase *ethnic group* is calculated to provide the necessary corrective to this erroneous viewpoint by eliminating the question-begging emphases of the biologistic bias on purely physical factors and differences, and demanding that the question of definition be left open until the necessary scientific research and answers are available. The emphasis is shifted to the fact that man is a uniquely cultural creature as well as a physical organism, and that under the influence of human culture the plasticity of man, both mentally and physically, is greatly increased—indeed, to such an extent as to lead anthropologists to the creation of races upon the basis of physical traits which were subsequently discovered to be due to cultural factors, as, for example, the head forms of the so-called Armenoid and Dinaric "races."

Here, too, reply may be made to those who may object that the phrase *ethnic group* is too reminiscent of the cultural. But this is precisely why the phrase is so well found. The Greek word *ethnos* originally meant a number of people living together, and subsequently came to be used in the sense of a tribe, group, nation, or people. In modern times the term "ethnic" has occasionally been used to refer to a group identified by ties both of race and of nationality. This is pretty much what the phrase *ethnic group* ought to be taken to mean in the sense given in our description of an ethnic group.

If it be said that what the student of man's variety is interested in is the way in which human groups came to be what they are, and that for this reason it is the biological facts and mechanisms in which he must be chiefly interested, the answer must be made that anyone who believes this must be disabused of his belief as quickly as possible. For it must be emphasized again that man is not merely a physical organism but a *human* being who as a member of

a cultural group has been greatly influenced by his culture.
Human populations have had a remarkable assortment of
marriage or breeding regulations, for instance, varying
standards of social selection, different kinds of social barriers, mobility, and similar variables, all of which have
probably played an appreciable part in the evolution of
ethnic differences. These are the very kinds of factors
which are most neglected by those who come to the study
of man with a biologistic bias. It would for such students
of man, especially those who come in from the nonhuman
biological fields, as well as for the layman, be a great advantage to be required to look at the problem of human
variety from the viewpoint of the ethnic group rather than
from that of "race." Where man is concerned the biologist,
like the layman, needs to add a cultural dimension to his
horizons. This is what the phrase *ethnic group* will help
him to do.

The conception of an ethnic group is quite different
from that which is associated with the term "race." The
phrase *ethnic group* represents a different way of looking
at populations, an open, non-question-begging way, a ten-
tative, noncommittal, experimental way, based on the new
understanding which the sciences of genetics and anthropology have made possible. A term is discontinued, retired,
but another is not merely substituted for it; rather a new
conception of human populations is introduced replacing
the old one, which is now dropped, and a term or phrase
suitable to this new conception is suggested. The old conception is *not* retained and a new name given to it, but a
new conception is introduced under its own name. That is
a very different thing from a mere change in names. It is
important to be quite clear upon this point, for the *new
conception* embraced in the phrase *ethnic group* renders
the possibility of the development of "ethnic group prej-

udice" quite impossible, for as soon as the nature of this conception is understood it cancels the possibility of any such development. It is a noncontaminating neutral concept.

To conclude and summarize: The advantages of the phrase *ethnic group* are: first, while emphasizing the fact that one is dealing with a distinguishable group, this noncommittal phrase leaves the whole question of the precise status of the group on physical and other grounds open for further discussion and research; second, it recognizes the fact that it is a group which has been subject to the action of cultural influences; and third, it eliminates all obfuscating emotional implications.

As for the suggested dropping or the restricted or suspended use of the term "race," there are many parallels for this in science. Possibly the most striking one in recent years is the dropping of the term "instinct" by psychologists for similar reasons to those which make the term "race" undesirable.[62] Similarly, in anthropology the term "savage" has been completely dropped, while the term "primitive" as referring to living peoples is largely being abandoned in favor of the term "nonliterate" for much the same reason, namely, the inaccuracy of the earlier terms, and hence their unsuitability. In biology the term "unit character" as erroneously referring to single genes as determining single characters or traits, has been for ever banished from the scientific vocabulary. Retardative concepts like "phlogiston" of eighteenth-century chemistry have been dropped never to be re-adopted. It may be that the terms "instinct" and "race" may someday be shown to have more than the merely verbal validity of common usage, but until that time it would be more in accordance with the scientific spirit to declare a moratorium on the use of the term "race."

PARAGRAPH 7

N ow, what has the scientist to say about the groups of
mankind which may be recognized at the present
time? Human races can be and have been differently classified by different anthropologists, but at the present time
most anthropologists agree in classifying the greater part
of present-day mankind into three major divisions, as follows:

> The Mongoloid Division
> The Negroid Division
> The Caucasoid Division

The biological processes which the classifier has here embalmed, as it were, are dynamic, not static. These divisions
were not the same in the past as they are at present, and
there is every reason to believe that they will change in
the future.

M ost cases," William James once remarked, "are mixed cases, and we should not treat our classifications with too much respect."[63] Actually, what the anthropologist is largely limited to doing is to describe populations and *attempt* to classify them. There have been innumerable classifications, mostly based on external physical traits. In modern times most anthropologists agree that there are three large stocks, divisions, or major groups into which all the "races" of mankind fall. The preferred term today for these divisions is *major groups*. This is the term we shall use here.

A major group of mankind may be defined as a complex or collection of populations or ethnic groups characterized by a relative similarity of physical characters which in combination serve to distinguish the members of that major group from the members of other major groups. For example, the dark skin color of the Negroids, tightly curled hair, and everted lips, together constitute a combination of characters which serves to distinguish the complex of populations possessing these traits from all other populations.

An ethnic group is a population more or less distinguished from other populations within the same division by the possession of one or more distinguishing traits.

The major groups which have been recognized by anthropologists have been described as follows:

THE MONGOLOID MAJOR GROUP

Inhabitants chiefly of northern, central, and southeastern Asia, embracing the Philippines, Malaysia, the East Indies, and the Americas, the Mongoloids are, anthropologically, perhaps the least known of the varieties of man.

The Mongoloids are characterized by lank, straight black hair on the head with fewer hairs per square centimeter than is present on the head of Whites. Body hair is relatively sparse. The skin has a faintly yellowish tinge, and a fold of skin overhanging the inner angle of the eye opening—the "epicanthic fold"—is present in most, though not in all, Mongoloids.

THE NEGROID MAJOR GROUP

This major group consists of three subgroups, (1) the African Negroids, (2) the Oceanic Negroids of the territory of New Guinea and the great group of islands extending to the east all the way to the Fiji Islands, and (3) the Negroids of Southeastern Asia, including the Andamanese of the Bay of Bengal, the Semang of the Malay Peninsula and East Sumatra, and the Aeta of the Philippines.

The Negroids exhibit a typically dark brown skin, which is often black, and in some groups yellowish brown. Head hair varies from tightly curled to pepper-corn (sparsely distributed tufts) and as a rule there is a marked paucity of hair over the rest of the body. The head tends to be long, the nose usually broad, frequently flattish with wide nostrils, the lips usually thick and everted, and there is a slight forward projection of the upper jaw (prognathism).

THE CAUCASOID MAJOR GROUP

This major group of mankind is often called "White." The term is not an altogether accurate one because the division includes many people of dark skin color, such as many of the peoples of India and also the Australian aborigines, the latter sometimes being placed in a special subgroup called the Archaic Caucasoid. The reason for giving this major group the name "Caucasoid" originates in the choice made by Blumenbach (1752-1840) the father of physical anthropology, who in the late eighteenth century described and named the type from a female skull whose beauty had much impressed him. The skull came from Georgia in the Caucasus, and it seemed to him to typify the cranial characters of the group.

Head hair, in varying degrees, is usually wavy, but ranges from silky straight to various degrees of curliness. It is never woolly, rarely frizzly, and is never as coarse or as sparsely distributed as in Mongoloids. The hair on the face and over the rest of the body in males is usually well developed. Skin color varies from white to dark brown. The nose is comparatively narrow and projecting, being relatively high at both root and bridge. The cheek bones are generally not prominent, and the lips tend to be thin.

PARAGRAPH 8

M any sub-groups or ethnic groups within these divisions have been described. There is no general agreement upon their number, and in any event most ethnic groups have not yet been either studied or described by the physical anthropologists.

W e give here a brief synoptic classification of the ethnic groups of mankind upon which most anthropologists agree. For a more extended account of these ethnic groups the reader may consult the works listed under reference 30, page 252.

THE MAJOR AND ETHNIC GROUPS OF MAN

MAJOR GROUP: MONGOLOID

   CLASSICAL MONGOLOIDS

Ethnic Group: An undetermined number of ethnic groups in the older populations of Tibet, Mongolia, China, Korea, Japan, and Siberia, including such tribes as the *Buriats* east and west of Lake Baikal, the *Koryak* of northern Siberia, the *Gilyak* of northernmost Sakhalin and the mainland north of the Amur estuary (who appear to have mixed with the Ainu), and the *Goldi* on the lower Amur and Ussuri.

ARCTIC MONGOLOIDS

Ethnic Group: *a. Eskimo:* extreme northeast of Asia, Arctic coast of North America, Greenland. The type includes the Aleuts of the Aleutian Islands, and the Reindeer and coastal Chukchee of northeastern Siberia.

      b. Evenki or true *Tungu* (Americanoid): Mongolia, Siberia, Asiatic highlands north of the Himalayas.

      c. Kamchadale: Kamchatka.

      d. Samoyed: Kola Peninsula, White Sea and Yenisei regions.

AMERICAN INDIANS

Ethnic Groups: An undetermined number of ethnic groups of North, Middle, Central, and South America.

INDO-MALAYS

Ethnic Group: *a.* Indonesian: Southern China, Indo-China, Burma, Thailand, interior of Malay Archipelago.

      b. Malay: in addition to Indonesian distribution, Malay Peninsula, Dutch East Indies, Philippines, Okinawa, and adjacent islands.

MAJOR GROUP: NEGROID

AFRICAN NEGROES

Ethnic Group: *a. True Negro:* West Africa, Cameroons, and Congo.

      b. Half-Hamites: East Africa and East Central Africa.

      c. Forest Negro: Equatorial and Tropical Africa.

   d. "Bantu-speaking Negroids": Central and Southern Africa.

   e. Nilotic Negro: Eastern Sudan and Upper Nile Valley.

   f. Bushman: Southern Angola and Northwest Africa.

OCEANIC NEGROIDS

Ethnic Group: *a. Papuan:* New Guinea.

   b. Melanesian: Melanesia.

AFRICAN PYGMIES OR NEGRILLOS

Ethnic Group: *a. African Pygmy or Negrillo:* Equatorial Africa.

ASIATIC PYGMIES OR NEGRITOS

Ethnic Group: *a. Andamanese:* Andaman Islands.

   b. Semang: Central region of Malay Peninsula, and East Sumatra.

   c. Philippine Negritos: Philippine Islands.

OCEANIC PYGMIES OR NEGRITOS

Ethnic Group: *a. New Guinea Pygmy:* New Guinea.

MAJOR GROUP: CAUCASOID

Ethnic Group: *a. Basic Mediterranean:* Borderlands of the Mediterranean Basin.

   b. Atlanto-Mediterranean: Middle East, eastern Balkans, East Africa, Portugal, Spain, British Isles.

   c. Irano-Afghan Mediterranean: Iran, Afghanistan, parts of India, Arabia, and North Africa.

   d. Nordic: Central Europe, Scandinavia, and neighboring regions.

   e. East Baltic: Eastern Baltic regions.

   f. Lapp: Northern Scandinavia, Kola Peninsula.

   g. Alpine: France along the Alps to Russia.

   h. Dinaric: Eastern Alps from Switzerland to Albania, Asia Minor, and Syria.

   i. Armenoids: Asia Minor.

   j. Hamites: North and East Africa.

   k. Indo-Dravidians: India and Ceylon.

   l. Polynesians: Polynesia (Central Pacific)

SUBGROUP: AUSTRALOIDS OR ARCHAIC CAUCASOIDS

 Ethnic Group: *a. Australian:* Australia.

   b. Veddah: Ceylon.

   c. Pre-Dravidian: India.

   d. Ainu: Japan, Hokkaido (Yezo), and Sakhalin Islands.

So much, then, for the classification of the ethnic groups of man. A word in conclusion: it should be remembered that the varieties of mankind have been far from adequately studied, and that the classification given above represents but an arbitrary and temporary convenience which is subject to considerable refinement and modification. It is designed to enable the reader to appreciate better certain broad facts, but not in any way to cause him to become fixed in his views.

PARAGRAPH 9

Whatever classification the anthropologist makes of man, he never includes mental characteristics as part of those classifications. It is now generally recognized that intelligence tests do not in themselves enable us to differentiate safely between what is due to innate capacity and what is the result of environmental influences, training and education. Whenever it has been possible to make allowances for differences in environmental opportunities, the tests have shown essential similarity in mental characters among all human groups. In short, given similar degrees of cultural opportunity to realize their potentialities, the average achievement of the members of each ethnic group is about the same. The scientific investigations of recent years fully support the dictum of Confucius (551-478 B.C.): "Men's natures are alike; it is their habits that carry them far apart."

Anthropologists of an earlier period *did* include mental characteristics as criteria of "racial" distinctiveness, but with the growth of modern knowledge of the peoples of the world, it soon became apparent that the mental differences between people living in different groups were due not so much to innate as to cultural factors. Hence, mental differences were dropped by all scientists as criteria which were in any way usable in the classification of mankind.

It will be noted that Paragraph 9 does not say that there are no differences in the innate potentialities for mental development among the ethnic groups of man. The problem has not yet been exhaustively investigated by scientists for anyone truthfully to be able to make such a statement. It is difficult to disentangle the innate genetic from the environmental factors in analyzing the intelligence of an individual. Intelligence tests largely measure the effects of social experience and training on some of the genetic potentialities of the person. Intelligence tests simply do not enable us to differentiate between what is due to innate capacity and what is the result of environmental influences, even when these tests are applied to a group of individuals who have had more or less the same environmental opportunities.

Even if tests free of cultural bias were available—and they are not, the fact that every ethnic group has had, and continues to have a significantly different history of experience, would alone be sufficient to make it impossible to differentiate between the effects of innate capacity and those of environmental opportunity. We therefore do not derive very much help from intelligence tests in attempts to discover whether there are any ethnic group differences in innate potentialities for intelligence. The evidence yielded by the analysis of intelligence tests indicates, in Professor Otto Klineberg's words, "That in all probability the range of inherited capacities in two different ethnic groups is just about identical."[64]

With rather monotonous regularity there appear, at almost predictable intervals, elaborate studies which purport to show that certain racial, ethnic, or social groups of other kinds are, on the whole, poorer learners and achievers than the group to which the investigator happens to belong. Such reports invariably suffer the same eventual fate. They are lauded by those who prefer to believe what these studies purport to demonstrate, and are severely criticized and condemned by the experts. Following a period of fervid discussion in the press, and partisan misuse in legislative houses, the ensuing controversies thus engendered gradually die down and the whole sorry business is finally consigned to the archives where such reports are deposited. In the meantime such reports give aid and comfort to racists and segregationists, fundamentalists, people who should know better, and they serve further to fortify in their citadels of infallibility the half-educated, and those who have been educated beyond their intelligence.

The latest work of this class is by Arthur B. Jensen, Professor of Educational Psychology at the University of California, Berkeley. In a study entitled "How Much Can We Boost IQ and Scholastic Achievement?" published in the Winter 1969 issue of the *Harvard Educational Review,* Jensen argues that it is "a not unreasonable hypothesis that genetic factors are strongly implicated in the average Negro-white intelligence difference."[65] Jensen then proceeds to show what everyone has known ever since the initiation of intelligence testing that Blacks on the average do not do as well on such tests as Whites. As others have done before him, Jensen attributes this difference largely to the operation of genetic factors, believing as he does that the IQ test constitutes the best available method of measuring the genetic contribution to intelligence. Jensen equates intelligence with the ability measured by IQ tests, and this ability he considers to be largely inherited, a matter of genes and brain structure. This leads him to the conclusion that no amount of compensatory education or forced exposure to any form of education or culture will improve that intelligence substantially. In brief, whatever it is that IQ tests measure is, according to Jensen, intelligence. Furthermore, according to him, intelligence is largely genetically determined.

It has, I believe, with greater force been suggested that what IQ tests really measure is the intelligence of those who believe that IQ tests measure intelligence. I think there is more to be said for this suggestion than for that which proposes that IQ tests largely measure genetic intelligence, for the facts, derived from innumerable independent studies, indicate that what IQ tests measure is very far removed from the genetic potentials for intelligence; that what IQ tests measure represents the expression of the interaction between those genetic potentials and the nutritional, socioeconomic, emotional, motivational, and schooling experience of the individual.[66]

One wonders whether those who are so ready to settle for the genetic factor as the principal cause of the differences in IQ between Blacks and Whites, would also hold that the enormous overall differences, at every age level, in morbidity and mortality rates between these two groups are also due to genetic factors? Whatever their view might be the evidence is overwhelming that, with few exceptions, these differences are due to social factors.[67]

Why is it that these racial ideologists refuse to acknowledge, even to consider, that social factors may be the principal causes responsible for the differences in learning abilities of different "racial" groups? Learning ability is highly correlated with social class within the same ethnic group.[68] What the racists fail to understand is that in man "race" is for all practical purposes a social concept and an institution, a special form of social class, a caste status, and that as such it is subject to all the influences and consequences that flow from that fact.[69]

That a significant genetic element contributes to the basic intelligence potential of every individual is beyond dispute. It should, however, be clear that like every other genetic potential the development of intelligence is, perhaps more than any other trait, dependent upon the kind of environmental stimulations to which it is exposed. Instead of dismissing such environmental factors as unimportant in order to sustain even the veriest semblance of his theory Jensen should have carefully investigated the possible effects of such environmental factors upon IQ test results. This he conspicuously failed to do, and for this reason alone his claims would have to be wholly rejected. To assign, as he does, a good 80 per cent of an individual's intelligence to genetic factors and a mere 20 per cent to environmental influences, constitutes not only a scientifically groundless assumption but also a wholly indefensible one. For there exists a vast body of scientific evidence which indicates not that either genetic potentials or environmental ones are more important than the other, but that both are of the greatest importance for the adequate development of intelligence.

The effect of malnutrition upon the development of intelligence, as well as its detrimental effects upon brain development, are now well established.[70] Equally well established is the damage done by unfavorable socioeconomic factors upon the development of intelligence.[71] The universal conclusion of all the relevant studies is that no matter what the genetic potentials for intelligence may be in the individual, the expression of those potentials will be significantly influenced by his total environment. Poverty as such is not necessarily either a necessary or a sufficient condition in the production of intellectual deficits, for if nutrition is adequate and the home cultural environment is adequate, the child will suffer no handicapping effects. But if nutrition is poor, health care inadequate, housing debasing, family income low, family disorganization endemic, discipline anarchic, ghettoization more or less complete, personal worth constantly diminished, aspirations consistently frustrated, as well as numerous other environmental handicaps, then one may expect the kind of failures in intellectual development that are so often gratuitously attributed to genetic factors. Those who make such attributions fail to understand how dependent the development of intelligence is upon the obverse of such conditions of privation, frustration, and hopelessness. When the effects of such postnatal environmental factors are combined with the adverse effects of prenatal ones, there emerges a continuum of psychosocial, as well as psychophysical, casualty, which makes it utterly nonsensical to compare casualties of such environments with the products of average middle-class environments by whom and on whom IQ tests were devised. It is not simply the culture of poverty or even the poverty of culture or any one single factor, but the combination of many socioenvironmental factors, which produces the sociogenic deficits so easily attributed to genetic factors. As Gladys Schwesinger pointed out in the conclusion to her book on *Heredity and Environment* in 1931, "The problem of heredity and environment is not a general problem, but is specific to each individual, to each of his characteristics, and to each environment." In the development of so complex an ability as intelligence, making every allowance for possible differences in genetic endowment, the environment is of paramount importance. Just as one learns to speak with the vocabulary, imagery, and accent according to the environmental influences that have been operative upon one, so one learns the vocabulary, imagery, and accent of intelligence, in accordance with the environmental influences with which one has interacted. As Bodmer and Cavalli-Sforza have put it, "Any given test . . . depends on the ability acquired at a given age, which is inevitably the result of the combination of innate ability and the experience of the subject. Intelligence tests are, therefore, at most tests of achieved ability."[72] And that is precisely the point. One has to learn to learn, and if the conditions are unfavorable for such learning one may learn not to learn. If seriously handicapping impediments are placed in the way of the individual's development of any capacity he will to that extent simply fail to achieve the ability to learn, for abilities are trained capacities, and capacities, to develop as abilities, require training. Limiting environments impose limits upon the development of abilities. In the matter of problem-solving, that is to say, intelligence, Harlow found that rhesus monkeys subjected to ambiguous rewards for tasks performed, so that no specific perceptual clues were available to the animals, were nowhere nearly as effective problem-solvers as those in the control group who were consistently rewarded. Harlow thus showed that the learning sets which make insight possible do not come ready-made, but must be acquired, and that once acquired they increase the capacity of the organism to solve certain problems.[73] Thompson and Heron have shown that pet-reared dogs in a variety of situations behave more intelligently than their litter-mates who have been caged for the first eight months of their lives.[74] All animals thus far studied show the effects of early experience or deprivation in much the same ways.[75]

Bennett, Rosenzweig, and Diamond have shown that exposure of rats to different environments—enriched, colony, or impoverished—leads to characteristic changes in wet and dry weight of samples of rat brain, in enzymatic activity, and in depth of cerebral cortex. Impoverished animals were caged singly, colony animals two or three per cage, and enriched animals ten or twelve per larger cage, with toys. In all respects, dry weight, depth of cerebral cortex, enzymatic activity, and problem solving behavior were increased in the animals exposed to an enriched environment as compared with standard colony and rats exposed to impoverished environments.[76] In mice Henderson found that an enriched environment resulted in an increased brain weight.[77]

One must be careful about extrapolating findings on other animals to man, but since the internal consistency of the evidence for other animals fully agrees with that obtained in studies of man, there can be little doubt that for the development of innumerable behavioral traits, but especially for the development of intelligence, the stimulation of certain kinds of social experience is indispensably necessary.[78] It is experience of an encouraging kind, as contrasted to experience of a discouraging kind, the experiences of an advantaging kind that count, as contrasted with those of a disadvantaging kind.

When we consider the complexity of the factors operating upon the child, the sociogenic brain damage done in man must be very considerable indeed, for there can be no question that it is brain damage when size, weight, failure of gray matter development, and enzymatic activity of the brain are the effects of a socially impoverished environment.

Jensen so completely fails to understand the nature of these disadvantaging conditions that he actually believes that the children of Blacks and Whites of similar income level enjoy equal cultural and other advantages. Hence, since these children enjoy similar environmental experiences, the difference in IQ test results, according to Jensen, must be due to genetic factors. What Jensen fails to understand is that income level alone does not determine the quality of cultural background, and that it is quite unsound to equate the two. There is no income level at which Blacks enjoy the same basic opportunities as Whites. By "basic opportunities" (see pp. 203-13) we mean a sustaining cultural background of stimulation which encourages

the growth and development of aspirations for achievement, a cultural background in which one does not suffer
from malnutrition of the body or of the spirit, in which
one has not suffered serious emotional, economic, social,
and educational privations, but to which, in most of these
respects a positive rather than a negative sign is attached.

The truth is that at no time have Blacks of any income
group enjoyed anything approaching equal basic opportunities with Whites. It is, therefore, quite unsound to
attribute to genetic factors what may well be due to environmental ones.[79] What is quite certain is that IQ's vary
with environmental experience. It is, for example, well
known that American Indians in general test out at about
80 points. But when oil is discovered on Indian land there
follows a spectacular rise in Indian IQ's. There is nothing
mysterious about this: the oil simply facilitates the lubrica-
tion of intelligence potentials by making the conditions
available which enable Indian children to enjoy a social
and economic environment similar to that of White children. Under such conditions among the Osage Indians of
Oklahoma, for example, Rohrer found that on one test,
the Goodenough "Draw-a-Man" test the White children
scored an average of 103 IQ points, and the Indian children 104. On a second test, using language, the White
children scored 98, the Indian children 100.[80]

Garth found that a group of Indian children living in
White foster homes obtained an average IQ of 102, which
is quite a significant advance over the usual American
Indian IQ of 80. The brothers and sisters of this group
still living on the reservation scored an average IQ of
87.5.[81]

Clearly the environmental differences were principally
responsible for the differences in the scores of these chil-

dren. There is no question of brain damage here, simply a difference in environment. Nor, for that matter, was a difference in genetic intelligence involved, for clearly that is not what these test results reflected. What they reflected was *a difference in environmental experience acting upon genetic potentials for intelligence, the ability to respond to IQ challenges*. It is not that the lower-testing siblings were any less intelligent than their higher-testing siblings, but that they were less experienced in the requirements necessary to meet the challenges of those tests.

Cooper and Zubek, in an interesting experiment, have shown how in different genetic lines different environments may serve either to develop or depress problem-solving capacities. These investigators used two lines of rats whose ability to find their way through a maze had been specially selected by selective breeding. When rats from the "bright" and "dull" lines were raised for a whole generation in a restricted environment which differed from the normal laboratory environment, no differences between the lines could be found. The bright and the dull performed at the same level. When both were raised in the same stimulating environment, both did almost equally well. In a normal environment bright rats made 120 errors, whereas the dull ones made 168. In a restricted environment both made about 170 errors, but in a stimulating environment the bright made 112 while the dull made 120, 48 errors less than in a normal environment.[82]

The power of the environment is clearly very considerable indeed, and the earlier it affects the developing organism the more substantive are its effects. Where the social stimuli are deficient mental development will be impaired and the ability to learn detrimentally affected. Tests of abilities of any sort unless they take such factors into consideration are worse than worthless, they are in their social effects capable of great damage. Hence, the importance of a thorough examination of the conditions under which such tests are conducted.

We do not know, but there may exist interesting differences in the distribution of genes for certain behavioral traits. From a theoretical point of view behavioral differences due to genes could come about by the same genetic mechanisms as were described in the discussion of Paragraph 1. As a matter of fact, there exists no definite evidence of such differences. In any event, such differences would be of small importance compared to the large differences within human populations. Professor Theodosius Dobzhansky and I have, as a matter of fact, shown there is very good reason to believe that, in the evolution of man, it was not the development of particular traits which was of adaptive value so much as the development of the general trait or rather complex of traits, which may be summed up in the word "plasticity." Hence, such differences as may exist between the ethnic groups of man are likely to be slight.[88]

It cannot be too strongly emphasized that such differences are not, *now,* known to exist between any ethnic groups of man. What we, *in fact,* find is that when the members of different groups are afforded similar opportunities for mental development the range of inherited capacities appears to be similar in all such groups. This should constitute pretty strong evidence that, in their innate potentialities for intelligence or other mental characteristics, the ethnic groups of mankind are fundamentally alike.

Where error and confusion have arisen in the past, they have come from attributing to genetic factors the mental differences which *appear* to distinguish different ethnic groups of man. Since these ethnic groups differ physically from one another the "obvious" conclusion drawn was that the mental differences were associated with the physical differences. The fact that these ethnic groups showed marked differences in cultural achievement was assumed to be due to the same supposed physical or genetic differences. The fact was overlooked that the differences in culture may be responsible for the mental differences, and that the differences in culture are not produced by innate factors, but are due to the differences in the history of cultural experience which each ethnic group has undergone. Too often effects were confused with causes.

What is today overwhelmingly clear is that certainly most, possibly all, of the undoubted cultural differences which exist between the ethnic groups of man have no genetic basis, but can be accounted for by differences in environmental influences, history, and opportunity. Human nature, as we observe it, represents the adaptation of the group, and of every individual comprising the group, to the total environment. The processes which men exhibit as behavior represent their adaptive responses to the environment, and their behavior will differ in accordance with the differences of the environment to which they have had to adjust, or, in other words, in which they have been conditioned. Man's habits of behavior are functions of his learned adjustments of his needs and potentialities to his environment. And environments, for ethnic groups, present an almost bewildering variety. Hence, Confucius' remark, "Men's natures are alike; it is their habits carry them far apart."

PARAGRAPH 10

The scientific material available to us at present does not justify the conclusion that inherited genetic differences are a major factor in producing the differences between the cultures and cultural achievements of different peoples or groups. It does indicate, however, that the history of the cultural experience which each group has undergone is the major factor in explaining such differences. The one trait which above all others has been at a premium in the evolution of man's mental characters has been educability, plasticity. This is a trait which all human beings possess. It is, indeed, a species character of Homo sapiens.

The question is often asked, "Why is it, since all ethnic groups have had an equal amount of time in which to develop culturally, that there are such great differences between so many of them in cultural development. Surely, the differences are due to innate capacity for development?"

The answer is that time, as such, is a wholly irrelevant factor. Supposing you and I had never been taught to read. Supposing that we live to be a hundred years of age in an illiterate state, can you imagine what our state of cultural development would be like? We should be cut off from almost all those things which make an educated modern man. We would, in short, be illiterates, and the hundred years we had lived would have made very little, if any, difference to our state of illiteracy. Time is irrelevant. What is relevant is the history of our cultural experience.

As it is with individuals, so it is with peoples. When human beings are brought up in an American environment they become Americans, whether their parents were originally Italian, Irish, English, French, German, Japanese, Chinese, or what not. By culture they are Americans because they were "culturized" in an American cultural environment, even though they may have been considerably influenced by the cultural heritage of their parents. There are many records of White children who were captured by American Indians and brought up as such who, as adolescents and as adults, were completely indistinguishable from Indians, except, sometimes, in physical appearance, and seldom even then.[83] Similarly White children brought up by Chinese,[84] and American Indian children brought up as Whites,[85] exhibit the cultural traits of the environment in which they were culturally conditioned. Their "ethnic group genes" seem to make no difference whatsoever to their ability to acquire any kind of culture. Furthermore, their ethnic affiliation does not seem ever to express itself in any recognizable elements of the culture or cultures with which their ethnic group may be associated. Ethnic group *cultural* genes simply do not exist. In addition, no ethnic group possesses any genes which set limits upon the acquisition of any culture by any of its members.

The reason why the American Indian has not, on the whole, acquired the culture of the Whites is that he has been segregated from that culture on reservations largely cut off from the main current of American life. As someone once put it, 'the trouble with the Red Indian is that he has been tied up with too much red tape.'

Similarly, the American Negro has to a large extent been refused admittance to full participation in American culture, and informed that there is no point to his striving to attain any of the desirable places in that culture because these are "for Whites only."

The Australian aboriginal, where he has not been detribalized, is still an Australian aboriginal living in an early Stone Age phase of cultural development, knowing no agriculture or husbandry, having no permanent habitation, and wandering as a nomad over his tribal territory. How is it that he remains so "primitive" in an age of cultural progress? The answer is that the Australian aboriginal has made a perfectly adequate adaptation to his environment. The fact that he has neither television nor jet planes, nor yet an atom bomb, is due largely to the fact that his own cultural history has been of a sort which has led to the preservation, relatively unaltered, of a way of life fully calculated to meet the needs of a group living by hunting and food gathering in a desert or semi desert environment. No more and no less. Isolated from virtually all cultural contact with other peoples for no one knows how many millennia, the Australian aborigines, on their island, preserve a form of culture which was, by and large, the stage of cultural development characteristic of all human groups not more than 20,000 years ago. The few Australian aborigines who have preserved this particular form or stage of cultural development have done so largely because they have been cut off from the fertilizing effects of cultural contacts with other peoples.

Had it not been for the fertilizing effects of such cross-cultural contacts, there is almost certainly no people which, under similar environmental conditions, would have developed very much beyond the Australian aborigines. The development of culture beyond those processes, which are necessary for gaining a living, the gathering and hunting of food, and the organization of the group as a cooperative unit, entails a variety of stimulations. Variety, it has been remarked, is the spice of life. It is also a necessary condition of cultural development, and variety of cultural contacts is what the Australian aborigines have not had and what the rest of the civilized world has, and that is the reason for the difference between the Australian aborigines—and any other people like them—and the remainder of the civilized world.[86] When Australian aborigines have been afforded an opportunity to acquire an education they have demonstrated their quality, frequently, with outstanding success.[87] The same is true for all nonliterate peoples of whom we have knowledge of this sort. In short, the indications are that it is because of differences in cultural experience, not because of differences in genetic structure, that groups differ culturally from one another. Man's evolutionary history, in addition to what we know of him at the present time, would suggest as much.

By means of his reasoning abilities man has achieved a mastery of the world's varying environments quite unprecedented in the history of organic evolution. The system of genes which has permitted the development of the specifically human mental capacities has thus become the foundation and most important influence in all subsequent evolution of the human stock. An animal becomes adapted to its environment by evolving certain genetically determined physical and behavioral traits. The adaptation of man consists chiefly in developing his inventiveness, a quality to which his physical heredity predisposes him and which his social heredity provides him with the means of realizing. To the degree to which this is so man is unique. As far as his mental responses to the world are concerned, he is largely emancipated from dependence upon inherited biological dispositions, uniquely improving upon the latter by the process of learning that which his social heredity (culture) makes available to him. Man possesses much more efficient means of achieving immediate or long-term adaptation than any other biological species—namely, through learned responses or novel inventions and improvisations.

If the mode of life of a species happens to be such that it is, of necessity, exposed to a wide range of environments, it becomes desirable to vary some structures and functions in accordance with the circumstances that confront an individual or a strain at a given time or place. Genetic structures which permit adaptive plasticity of traits become, then, obviously advantageous for survival and so are fostered by natural selection.

The social environments that human beings have created everywhere are notable not only for their extreme complexity but also for the rapid changes to which immediate adjustment is demanded. Adjustment occurs chiefly in the mental realm and has little or nothing to do with physical traits. In view of the fact that from the very beginning of human evolution the changes in the human environment have been not only rapid but diverse and manifold, genetic fixation of behavioral traits in man would have been decidedly unfavorable for the survival of individuals as well as of the species as a whole.

Success of the individual in most human societies has depended and continues to depend upon his ability rapidly to evolve behavior patterns which fit him to the kaleidoscope of the conditions he encounters. He is best off if he submits to some, compromises with some, rebels against others, and escapes from still other situations. Individuals who display a relatively greater fixity of response than their fellows suffer under most forms of human society and tend to fall by the way. Suppleness, plasticity, and, most important of all, ability to profit by experience and education are required. No other species is comparable to man in its capacity to acquire new behavior patterns and discard old ones in consequence of training. The survival value of this capacity is manifest, and therefore the possibility of its development through natural selection should be evident.

The genetically controlled plasticity of mental traits is, biologically speaking, the most typical and uniquely human characteristic. It is very probable that the survival value of this characteristic in human evolution has been considerable for a long time. Just when this characteristic first appeared is, of course, conjectural. The remains of prehistoric man's cultural activities indicate that the essentially human organization of the mental capacities emerged quite early in the evolution of man. However that may be, the possession of the gene system which conditions educability rather than behavioral fixity, is a common property of all living mankind. In other words, educability is truly a species trait of man, *Homo sapiens,* the animal which, beyond all others, is capable of learning and inventing.

The physical and, even more, the social environments of men who live in different countries are quite diversified. Therefore, it has often been argued, natural selection would be expected to differentiate the human species into local races differing in mental traits. Populations of different countries may differ in skin color, head shape, and other physical traits. Why, then, should they be alike in mental traits?

Arguments based on analogies are precarious, especially where evolutionary patterns are concerned. If human "races" differ in structural traits, it does not necessarily follow that they must also differ in mental ones. "Race" differences arise chiefly because of the differential action of natural selection on geographically separated populations. In the case of man, however, the structural and mental traits are quite likely to be influenced by selection in different ways.

The survival value of a higher development of mental capacities in man is obvious. Furthermore, natural selection seemingly favors such a development everywhere. In the ordinary course of events in almost all societies those persons are likely to be favored who show wisdom, maturity of judgment, and ability to get along with people— qualities which may assume different forms in different cultures. Those are the qualities of the plastic personality, not a single trait but a general condition which appears to have been at a premium in practically all human societies.

In human societies, with few exceptions, conditions have been neither rigid nor stable enough to permit the selective breeding of genetic types adapted to different statuses or forms of social organization. Such rigidity and stability do not obtain in any society. On the other hand, the outstanding fact about human societies is that they do change and do so more or less rapidly. The rate of change was possibly comparatively slow in earlier societies, as the rate of change in present-day, nonliterate societies may be, when compared to the rate characterizing Occidental societies. In any event, rapid changes in behavior are demanded of the person at all levels of social organization even when the society is at its most stable. Life at any level of social development in human societies is a pretty complex business, and it is met and handled most efficiently by those who exhibit the greatest capacity for adaptability, plasticity.

It is this very plasticity of his mental traits which confers upon man the unique position which he occupies in the animal kingdom. Its acquisition freed him from the constraint of a limited range of biologically predetermined responses. He became capable of acting in a more or less regulative manner upon his physical environment instead of being largely regulated by it. The process of natural selection in all climes and at all times has favored genetic types (genotypes) which permit greater and greater educability and plasticity of mental traits under the influence of the uniquely social environments to which man has been continuously exposed.

We conclude, then, that the effect of natural selection in man has probably been to render genetic differences in personality traits, as between individuals and particularly as between ethnic groups, relatively unimportant compared to their potentialities for adaptation and adjustment to all manner of conditions, compared, in other words, to their plasticity.[88]

PARAGRAPH 11

So far as temperament is concerned, there is no definite evidence that there exist inborn differences between human groups. There is evidence that whatever group differences of the kind there might be are greatly over-ridden by the individual differences, and by the differences springing from environmental factors.

E ven among those who believe in the equality of man so far as his native abilities are concerned, one often encounters the belief that there are, nevertheless, genuine inborn differences in temperament in different human groups. For instance, we hear of "the expansive and rhythm-loving Negro temperament," "the shut-in temperament of the American Indian," "the volatile temperament of the Mediterranean," and so on.

Temperament has been defined as the susceptibility to certain kinds of emotional response, or as the total affective aspect of the personality which includes feelings, emotions, moods, sentiments, attitudes, and their organization. Temperament, then, is the mood of a lifetime.

If it were true that there exist inborn temperamental differences between the ethnic groups of man, the differences ought to be welcomed as providing a greater diversity of possibilities of each ethnic group. The fact is, however, that all investigations which have thus far been conducted into the subject are quite inconclusive, but on the whole strongly point in the direction of there being no significant inborn differences in temperament between different ethnic groups. The differences observed seem to be as culturally determined as the expressive gestures which are characteristic of various groups.[89]

That culture plays a dominant role in the formation of temperament is apparent from such facts as the following. When "the expansive and rhythm-loving Negro" is brought up in England he becomes as composed and phlegmatic and as awkward rhythmically as is the average Englishman. It is an illuminating experience to listen to an English Negro jazzband and observe English Negroes dancing to and singing with it. Apparently the expression of one's emotions is as subject to the effects of training as are most other behavioral potentialities of the organism. White children captured by American Indians and brought up as such exhibited the "stolid" Indian temperament.[90] In a study of three different cultures Margaret Mead has shown us that in three different tribes of the same Papuan ethnic group there were marked and characteristic differences in temperament which were largely traceable to differences in the socializing or culturally conditioning processes peculiar to each culture.[91] Other anthropologists have demonstrated similar relationships for many other groups.[92]

Finally, the varieties of temperament, varying with each culture to some extent and changing often with time, which one encounters in the nations of Europe of the same ethnic stock, should constitute sufficient proof of the fact that temperament is largely conditioned by cultural factors.[93]

None of these facts, however, prove that there are no genetic factors involved in the development of a person's temperament or that there may not be genetic differences in the distribution of the genes affecting temperament in the different ethnic groups of man. What evidence there is indicates that whatever group differences of the kind there may be, are over-ridden by the individual differences, and by differences of environmental origin.

PARAGRAPH 12

As for personality and character, these may be considered raceless. In every human group a rich variety of personality and character types will be found, and there is no reason for believing that any human group is richer than any other in these respects.

B y personality is understood the sum of qualities and characteristics that constitute individuality.

By character we mean the sum of a person's mental and moral qualities.

Personality is the dynamic aspect of character.

What has been said about temperament applies equally to personality and character.[94] Here we may repeat the fact that while genes may be involved in the development of both personality and character, such genes appear to be similarly distributed in all populations of which we have any knowledge. Furthermore, the effects of the environment are provably substantial upon the development both of personality and character. Class and caste differences within the same society abundantly testify to that fact. Every group sets up its own cultural ideals for both personality and character. These ideals appear to be largely or wholly culturally determined, and most individuals in a given culture are trained to conform to them. Such ideals or standards and the training in them have nothing, so far as we know, to do with inborn determinants.[96] Again, when this has been said it also requires to be said that while genes are almost certainly involved in the development of the individual's personality and character it seems reasonably certain, on the basis of the evidence, that it is not genes which are the most important determiners of personality and character, but culture.

PARAGRAPH 13

With respect to race-mixture, the evidence points unequivocally to the fact that this has been going on from the earliest times. Indeed, one of the chief processes of race-formation and race-extinction or absorption is by means of hybridization between races or ethnic groups. Furthermore, no convincing evidence has been adduced that race-mixture of itself produces biologically bad effects. Statements that human hybrids frequently show undesirable traits, both physically and mentally, physical disharmonies and mental degeneracies, are not supported by the facts. There is, therefore, no biological justification for prohibiting intermarriage between persons of different ethnic groups.

A great many unfortunate myths have grown up about "race mixture." Let us examine these. We have already discussed the importance of hybridization in the evolution of man and his ethnic groups. By "race extinction" in the above paragraph is meant the disappearance of distinct ethnic groups by their merging into one another. By "race absorption" is meant the incorporation of one ethnic group by another, so that the incorporated group, as such, disappears without producing any marked physical alterations in the appearance of the absorbing ethnic group. An example of the first kind of "extinction," for which we have some suggestive evidence, is the merging of ethnic groups in prehistoric times which some scientists believe to have occurred, for example, in the Near East.[97] Such merging is suggested by the skeletal characters seen in the late Middle Pleistocene people of Mount Carmel, Palestine, who lived about 80,000 years or more ago. All living ethnic groups are probably the result of such mergings. In our own time the merging continues, as does the process of absorption. The absorption of the Polynesians and the Australian aborigines by Whites of other ethnic groups seems a matter of but a relatively short time. That Neanderthal man was absorbed by men of our own type is a practical certainty.

The notion that race mixture produces biologically bad effects is encountered not only among laymen but sometimes also among those who claim to have made a scientific study of the facts. But for those who are not concerned with proving a particular theory but are interested in discovering what the facts are, the story is quite clear.[98]

All the evidence which we have shows that mixtures between members of different ethnic groups never produce any structural disharmonies. The offspring of Negroid-White matings, Australian aboriginal-White matings, Mongoloid-White, and numerous others, are well known. So far as I know there is not a single recorded authenic case of morphological disharmony of any kind resulting from such matings. On the other hand, the offspring of such matings are usually biologically in every way harmonic and desirable types. Statements to the effect that when Blacks and Whites mate the offspring are physically inferior to both of the parents are quite false. It is said that the Black mother has difficulty in delivering the fetus of a White father because of the round head of the fetus and the narrow pelvic canal of the Black female. These statements are untrue in their entirety. The pelvic canal of the Black female is not normally narrow, and it would not matter what, within normal limits, the shape of the head of the fetus would be, because this is malleable enough to pass through the birth canal of any type of normal pelvis. Finally, mortality rates for offspring of mixed matings are no higher in the Black group than they are for unmixed matings.[99]

Is it necessary to mention all the other alleged disharmonies which are supposed to follow upon ethnic intermixture? "The large teeth of the one parent in the small jaws of the other," "the large upper jaw of one parent and the small lower jaw of the other," "the long arms of the one and the short arms of the other," and so on? If space permitted it would be helpful to do so and to examine them one by one, but all we can do here is to state that such disharmonies do not occur and that when, in the offspring of such matings, any abnormalities are observed, they are due not to racial factors but to those very same factors that produce similar conditions within some members of the same ethnic group. If one or other of the parents is genetically defective in some way some of the offspring may exhibit the defect—race has nothing to do with the matter.[100]

On the other hand, there are several functional traits such as Rh-negative blood types, sickle-cell anemia, and lack of resistance to tuberculosis, which may be transmitted through "race mixture." These traits occur in some ethnic groups but not in others. Crossing between them will serve to distribute the genes for these conditions in the populations which do not possess them or do not possess them in high frequencies. However, these genes have but slight biological functional disadvantages. Rh-negative genes in the mother are related to the absence of certain substances in the blood which are concerned with the manufacture of antibodies. In their absence such a mother mating with an Rh-positive male may have a number of babies who will die shortly before or shortly after birth. Most Mongoloids are free of this condition, about 16 per cent of Whites and 8 per cent of American Blacks carry the gene. Sickle-cell anemia occurs almost exclusively in Negroids or persons with some Negroid ancestry. Negroid peoples do not appear to be very resistant to tuberculosis.

The fact is, however, that modern civilization's understanding of the genetic mechanisms of these conditions makes it possible, in most cases, to prevent the development of these conditions, or if they develop, to treat them effectively.

Statements to the effect that the hybrid is inferior socially and mentally to both his parents, and that the decline of former high civilizations and powerful nations has been due to admixture with "inferior races," are not supported by the facts.

In most societies in which they are observed by those who are usually not disposed to judge them either fairly or sympathetically, the offspring of mixed unions are treated as "half-castes"; that is to say, as having a truncated status, which in practice means bearing the stigma of not being socially respectable, belonging neither to the one group nor to the other. To be placed in such an anomalous social position from birth can hardly be described as elevating. On the contrary, it is likely to wreck the lives of most of the persons placed in it. To be in such a position is to be in a state of social depression, to suffer the privation of the respect due to all human beings, to be deprived of those opportunities for human development which alone enable a human being to emerge as a relatively well-organized person.[101]

As Professor W. E. Castle of Harvard and the University of California has put it: "Since there are no biological obstacles to crossing between the most diverse human races, when such crossing does occur, it is in disregard of social conventions, race pride and race prejudice. Naturally therefore it occurs between antisocial and outcast

specimens of the respective races, or else between conquerors and slaves. The social status of the children is
thus bound to be low, their educational opportunities
poor, their moral background bad. . . . Does the half-
breed, in any community of the world in which he is
numerous, have an equal chance to make a man of himself,
as compared with the sons of the dominant race? I think
not. Can we then fairly consider him racially inferior just
because his racial attainments are less? Attainments imply
opportunities as well as abilities."[102]

When, indeed, the offspring of mixed unions are afforded
even a half-decent opportunity to develop as well as they
are under the circumstances able, they do as well as the
members of any group of human beings with equal opportunities.

Class and caste, and socioeconomic status are, in all
societies, highly correlated with social development and
intelligence of the individual.[103] This is perhaps nowhere
more impressively clear than with respect to the Black in
the United States. In the Northern states the Black has
enjoyed better social advantages of every kind than has
the Black in the South. The differences in social development, including intelligence, are markedly in favor of the
Northern Black. Not only this, the superior socioeconomic
advantages which many Northern Blacks enjoy as compared with those prevailing for many Whites in the South
is reflected in their superior performance in intelligence
and other social tests. This is clearly exhibited in the results of the analysis of intelligence tests administered to
Negro and White draftees during World War I.[104] Table I
sets out these findings. Beta tests were administered to
illiterates and semi-literates, and Alpha tests were administered to literates.

TABLE I

States of the Union in Which Blacks Did Better
Than Whites on Beta and Alpha Tests
From Ashley Montagu, 1945 [105]

Beta Tests		Alpha Tests	
BLACKS FROM THE STATE OF	DID BETTER THAN THE WHITES FROM THE FOLLOWING NUMBER OF STATES	BLACKS FROM THE STATE OF	DID BETTER THAN THE WHITES FROM THE FOLLOWING NUMBER OF STATES
Ohio	27	Ohio	9
Kansas	24	Illinois	7
New York	11	New York	5
Missouri	11	Indiana	2
Indiana	6		
Illinois	6		

The literate Blacks, when they did better on the tests than literate Whites, were from Northern states while their inferiors on the tests were always from Southern states. This largely held true for the illiterate tests. Marcuse and Bitterman have shown that the scores made on these tests are highly correlated with the yearly educational expenditures of the states from which the draftees were drawn as well as with the per capita income prevailing in those states. As these investigators remark, the conclusion is warranted that the scores on these tests reflect the strong influence of cultural factors associated with the socioeconomic levels of the states.[106]

As for the alleged degenerative effects of "race mixture" upon the development of nations, it has been shown that immediately prior to that great and magnificent efflorescence of culture in ancient Greece, "race mixture" had been proceeding rapidly.[107] The decline of Greek culture cannot be due to race mixture because the Greeks remain relatively unmixed since Athenian days; it may, on the other hand, be convincingly explained in terms of historical conditions. The tragic history of political anarchy, war, massacre, social disorganization, conquest and oppression which has been the lot of the Greek people during the last two thousand years, is more than sufficient to explain the decline of Greek civilization. "Racial" factors have had nothing to do with it. And so it is with all other civilizations which have suffered a decline.

Indeed, if it were true that "race mixture" results in decadence, man should have died out long ago or else sunk to the level of a deformed idiot, for he is one of the most highly hybridized animals on the face of the earth.

The fact is that far from having undesirable biological and social consequences, "race mixture" appears to result in desirable biological effects, and if there is involved an associated difference in culture, the mixture of cultural traditions usually results in much stimulating, novel, and enriching growth and development. It is from the mixing of cultural traditions that many of the major triumphs of civilization have come. It is certain that many of the biological triumphs of men have come from the mixing of "races" or ethnic groups. Hence, for all these reasons, there is no *biological* justification for prohibiting intermarriage between persons of different ethnic groups.

PARAGRAPH 14

T he biological fact of race and the myth of "race" should be distinguished. For all practical social purposes "race" is not so much a biological phenomenon as a social myth. The myth of "race" has created an enormous amount of human and social damage. In recent years it has taken a heavy toll in human lives and caused untold suffering. It still prevents the normal development of millions of human beings and deprives civilization of the effective cooperation of productive minds. The biological differences between ethnic groups should be disregarded from the standpoint of social acceptance and social action. The unity of mankind from both the biological and social viewpoints is the main thing. To recognize this and to act accordingly is the first requirement of modern man. It is but to recognize what a great biologist wrote in 1874: "As man advances in civilization, and small tribes are united into larger communities, the simplest reason would tell each individual that he ought to extend his social instincts and sympathies to all the members of the same nation, though personally unknown to him. This point being once *reached, there is only an artificial barrier to prevent his sympathies extending to the men of all nations and races." These are the words of Charles Darwin in "The Descent of Man" (2nd ed., 1874, pp. 187-188). And, indeed, the whole of human history shows that a cooperative spirit is not only natural to man, but more deeply rooted than any self-seeking tendencies. If this were not so we should not see the growth of integration and organization of his communities which the centuries and the millennia plainly exhibit.*

This paragraph states what should be self-evident after the discussions of the preceding pages. It states that there are two concepts of race: one is the biological fact of race which has already been defined and discussed (pages 37-71), and the other is the social concept of "race." The biological conception of race, in the terms in which we have already described it, is a fact. The social concept of "race" is a myth—that is, the notion that something called "race" is the prime determiner of all the important traits of the body and mind, of character and personality; and that this something called "race" is a fixed and unchangeable part of the germ plasm, which, transmitted from generation to generation, unfolds in each people as a typical expression of personality and culture. We have already set out the reasons why this social conception of "race" is false.

The truth of the biological conception of race must be affirmed. The falseness of the social conception of "race" must be carefully distinguished from the biological conception of race and denied the validity which is claimed for it by confrontation with the facts. The myth of "race" has demonstrated its harmfulness beyond the point at which it should be anywhere tolerated. It should be outlawed from the minds of all men.

There is nothing in the biological differences between the ethnic groups of men which calls for any social discrimination whatever. All human beings, no matter what their origins or ethnic affiliations may be, should be treated as persons in their own right, as members of the human family, who, after being separated for many years, are, in a contracting world, coming to live together again. We know that to live together men must cooperate. We know, too, that cooperation is the law of life, and that, as Darwin put it, there are only artificial barriers to prevent man's sympathies from extending to the men of all nations and races. Where such artificial barriers exist it should be our bounden obligation to our fellow men and to ourselves to see that they are discontinued.[108]

When men cooperate, they and their enterprises flourish and peace reigns. Man's attitudes toward his fellows are reflected back to him. As Lowy has said, "the idea of Society is essentially the *reflection and echo of your feelings* toward your fellowmen." [109] Man's inherent drives toward cooperation need but to be cultivated and intelligently handled for this world to be turned into what it could be.

PARAGRAPH 15

& Conclusions (16-20)

W e now have to consider the bearing of these statements on the problem of human equality. It must be asserted with the utmost emphasis that equality as an ethical principle in no way depends upon the assertion that human beings are in fact equal in endowment. Obviously individuals in all ethnic groups vary greatly among themselves in endowment. Nevertheless, the characteristics in which human groups differ from one another are often exaggerated and used as a basis for questioning the validity of equality in the ethical sense. For this purpose we have thought it worth while to set out in a formal manner what is at present scientifically established concerning individual and group differences.

16   In matters of race, the only characteristic which anthropologists can effectively use as a basis for classifications are physical and physiological.

17   According to present knowledge there is no proof that the groups of mankind differ in their innate mental characteristics, whether in respect of intelligence or temperament. The scientific evidence indicates that the range of mental capacities in all ethnic groups is much the same.

18 *Historical and sociological studies support the view that genetic differences are not of importance in determining the social and cultural differences between different groups of* Homo sapiens, *and that the social and cultural changes in different groups have, in the main, been independent of changes in inborn constitution. Vast social changes have occurred which were not in any way connected with changes in racial type.*

19 *There is no evidence that race-mixture as such produces bad results from the biological point of view. The social results of race-mixture whether for good or ill are to be traced to social factors.*

20 *All normal human beings are capable of learning to share in a common life, to understand the nature of mutual service and reciprocity, and to respect social obligations and contracts. Such biological differences as exist between members of different ethnic groups have no relevance to problems of social and political organization, moral life and communication between human beings.*

Paragraph 15 concerns the important matter of "race" and the living of the good life. The five paragraphs which follow briefly summarize what has been stated in the earlier paragraphs, and constitute the conclusions relating to what is, at present, scientifically established concerning individual and group differences. These conclusions require no further discussion; it may, however, be helpful to have some discussion of Paragraph 15.

What is asserted in Paragraph 15 is fundamental. Let us, then, be sure that we clearly understand what is there stated.

The bearing of the statements set out in the fourteen

preceding paragraphs on the problem of human equality should be clear: from the biological or the sociological viewpoints there is every good reason to regard all men as members of the human family and capable of leading the good life in love and brotherhood with all men.

The first clause of the Preamble of the United Nations *Universal Declaration of Human Rights*[110] makes "recognition of the inherent dignity and of the equal and inalienable rights of all members of the human family" as "the foundation of freedom, justice and peace in the world." And Article 1 states "all human beings are born free and equal in dignity and rights. They are endowed with reason and conscience and should act towards one another in a spirit of brotherhood."

This is what is meant in Paragraph 15 by "human equality." To repeat—for it cannot be repeated too often —by human equality we mean the recognition of the inherent dignity and of the equal and inalienable rights of all members of the human family. All the facts we have indicate that there is not a single biological or sociological datum which would in any way have any negative bearing upon the recognition of the universal truth of human equality as defined above. In biological endowment and in social opportunities for cultural development men differ from one another, but these differences from the ethical viewpoint, have no relation to human equality. No matter how much they may differ in endowment, whether genetic or social or both, all men are equal in dignity and in their rights. The conception of the equal rights of men stems from the fact that they are all equally men; no other fact can, or should, ever be permitted to annul this fact. There is nothing in the nature of any group which gives it less weight in the balance of equality than any other. "All

human beings are born free and equal in dignity and
rights." [111]

As Sidney Hook has pointed out, the principle of human
equality is not a description of fact concerning the physical
or intellectual nature of men. It is, rather, a prescription
or policy for human relations. It is a policy of equality of
concern and consideration for all men according to their
individual needs. A policy affording equal opportunities
to all men to realize their potentialities to the fullest, and
to make whatever contributions their capacities permit. [112]

Alleged or real ethnic differences, however conceived
or misconceived, cannot constitute a defensible ground
upon which to argue a case against the principle of human
equality. In any event it is a poor argument which attempts
to oppose the comparatively small number of differences
against the overwhelming number of likenesses which
characterize all men unexceptionally. It has already been
emphasized that the ethical principle of human equality
derives its force from the fact that all men are human
beings, whatever their physical differences. Differences in
physical appearance are not to be judged in terms of inequality in any sense. The physical differences between
men are all equal to the functions they were adaptively
developed to meet.

On biological grounds alone, then, there would be no
basis for questioning the validity of the equality of all
men. And in point of fact there can be no basis in the
physical characters of man for questioning the ethical
basis of equality. While human beings differ in endowment their likenesses are nevertheless substantial. The
very fact that men differ in endowment should make it
more necessary that they be afforded equal rights and
opportunities for development than would be the case

if they were all identical in endowment. Where the range of variability in endowment is as great as it is among human beings, even in the same family, more attention to the individual is necessary in order to discover how best his unique potentialities may be afforded the opportunity for development. But it must be repeated: Whatever the differences in physical characters or in endowment, the ethical principle of human equality applies to every human being—everywhere.

PARAGRAPH 21

Lastly, biological studies lend support to the ethic of universal brotherhood; for man is born with drives toward co-operation, and unless these drives are satisfied, men and nations alike fall ill. Man is born a social being who can reach his fullest development only through interaction with his fellows. The denial at any point of this social bond between man and man brings with it disintegration. In this sense, every man is his brother's keeper. For every man is a piece of the continent, a part of the main, because he is involved in mankind.

The findings of anthropologists concerning the physical and cultural evolution of men from the earliest times to the present day support to the full the belief in the unity, the universal brotherhood of man. There is a biological equality in difference, in much the same way as the musicians in an orchestra are equal even though they play different instruments. The musicians in an orchestra play together, in symphony, in cooperation. Each with his individual talent plays to the best of his ability to contribute to the perfection of the whole. The world of man may also be envisaged.

Modern scientific studies have revealed that man's drives are naturally directed toward cooperation with his fellow men, and that the reason why he frequently does not cooperate with his fellows is due to the distortion of his innate drives by the disordering life experience which he is so often made to undergo. Since these findings have but very recently been brought to the attention of the world, perhaps we had better consider them more at length here.

These findings lend further support to the ethic of human brotherhood.

Let us begin with a single typical example. When an experimenter removes individual cells some distance from their fellows, each separated cell immediately begins to make its way back to the group.[113] Innumerable examples of a similar kind could be cited which indicate the existence of some sort of social drive throughout the kingdom of living forms.[114] Whether we are dealing with fungi, bacteria, or higher plants and animals, the drive to form social groups is similar everywhere. Indeed, so far as man is concerned, the sense of mutuality and the trait of cooperativeness represent far stronger tendencies within him than combativeness and competitiveness.

The source of this social appetite may be traced to the way in which a living organism originates. All cells originate from other cells; it is impossible for them to originate in any other way. Whether reproduction is nonsexual or sexual, the process is always an interacting one between parent and developing new organism. The parent supplies the vital tissues to the new organism, and in the process of reproduction there are metabolic and other physiologic exchanges between them, before parent and offspring become independent of each other. This type of relationship, in varying degree, is characteristic of all plant and animal life.

The evidence indicates that the fundamentally social nature of all living things has its origin in this physiological relationship between parent and offspring; in the fact that each is for a time bound together with the other in an interactive association; in the fact that the life of either one or the other is, at some time, dependent upon the potential or actual being of the other. For example, when an amoeba has reached a certain size it can avoid death only by dividing, and this it does. The new organism is, at least during the period of division, entirely dependent upon the proper functioning of its parent. In this dependency we may perceive the origins of infant dependency in the higher animals and the very obvious social and, particularly in man, cultural consequences of that dependent relationship. In short, the universal fact of reproduction and all that it implies would appear to constitute the foundation and pattern of the social relationship which characterizes all living organisms.

This is as true of organisms composed of many cells as it is of organisms composed of a single cell. Cells, it would appear, which were originally separate, develop the habit of remaining attached, after division, to form a multicellular organism, as spores often do in the encysted envelope of the parent amoeba. As a result of their increasing ability to cooperate, such interactive cells develop specialized functions as well as increasingly complex relations. For this reason, a multicellular organism must be regarded as the expression of increasing cellular cooperation, in which the interdependent cooperating activities of its cellular masses function together, so that, at all times, the organism is able to function as a whole. Whatever the nature of the factors involved in the cooperation of cells in many-celled organisms, such cooperation exhibits the elements of a social act. And such acts represent the expression of a drive which had its origin in the relationship of parent cell and offspring cell.

The tendency of living things to form societies is coeval with life itself. No living organism is either solitary in its origin or solitary in its existence. Every organism from the simplest to the most complex is normally engaged in some sort of social life. The solitary animal is, in any species, an abnormal creature. The fact that such diverse groups as insects and mammals have developed highly cooperative forms of social life indicates, beyond any reasonable doubt, the existence in organic life of deep-seated potentialities toward cooperation and society.

The unconscious kind of cooperation which universally exists among simpler animals is even more developed among the more advanced forms. It is important to understand, in its full implications, the fact that this principle of cooperation appears to have governed the relations of organisms from the first. The notion that animals are in a constant state of warfare with one another, that "the struggle for existence" and "the survival of the fittest" are the two cardinal principles of "natural selection," is grossly one-sided and misleading. Although activities which may collectively be described as "the struggle for existence" do characterize the behavior of most animals, that "struggle" is not by any means to be understood in terms of combativeness. There are innumerable competitive forms of behavior, but these are complementary to forms of behavior which are dominantly cooperative.

In what might be called "the tough Darwinian period" of the last century, the concept of "the survival of the fittest," in its crudest form, dominated the thought of biologists and sociologists, with the consequence that although some biologists, and certainly Darwin himself, recognized the existence of cooperation, it was almost completely neglected in favor of the doctrine of the survival of the fittest. The few attempts which were made to state the case for cooperation were, for a time, somewhat slighted.

During the twentieth century much work has been done

on the biosocial activities of animals, with the result that today the principle of cooperation is in a fair way to becoming established as the most important factor in the survival of animal groups. Summing up the modern point of view, one of the leading workers in this field, Professor Warder C. Allee, writes: "After much consideration, it is my mature conclusion, contrary to Herbert Spencer, that the cooperative forces are biologically the more important and vital. The balance between the cooperative, altruistic tendencies and those which are disoperative and egoistic is relatively close. Under many conditions, the cooperative forces lose. In the long run, however, the group-centered, more altruistic drives are slightly stronger.

"If cooperation had not been the stronger force, the more complicated animals . . . could not have evolved from simpler ones, and there would have been no men to worry each other with their distressing and biologically foolish wars. While I know of no laboratory experiments that make a direct test of this problem, I have come to this conclusion by studying the implications of many experiments which bear on both sides of the problem and from considering the trends of organic evolution in nature. Despite many known appearances to the contrary, human altruistic drives are as firmly based on an animal ancestry as is man himself. Our tendencies toward goodness, such as they are, are as innate as our tendencies toward intelligence; we could do with more of both."[115]

The habit of thinking in terms of "the struggle for existence," by means of which, it is believed, the "fittest" are alone selected for survival while the weakest are ruthlessly condemned to extinction, is not only an incorrect view of the facts, but is a mode of thought which has done a considerable amount of harm. As Allee remarks, "Today, as in Darwin's time, the average biologist apparently still thinks of a natural selection which acts primarily on egoistic principles, and intelligent fellow thinkers in other disciplines, together with the much-cited man-in-the-street, cannot be blamed for taking the same point of view."[116]

Certainly, some aggressiveness exists in all living organisms, but there is also such a thing as a healthy, nonruthless aggressiveness. Moreover, there exist in every organism the strongest drives toward cooperative behavior. Some aggressiveness, some competitiveness, and some cooperativeness are to be observed in practically all animals. These forces operate not independently but together, and the evidence strongly indicates that, of them all, the drive for cooperation is the most dominant, and biologically the most important. The co-existence of so many different species of animals throughout the world constitutes eloquent testimony to the importance of that principle. It is probable that man owes more to the operation of this principle than to any other in his own biological and social evolution. Indeed, without this principle of cooperation, of sociability and mutual aid, the progress of organic life, the improvement of the organism, and the strengthening of the species, becomes utterly incomprehensible.

On the basis of the facts we may conclude that the more cooperatively the members of any group behave, the more harmonious the social organization of that group is likely to be. In 1944 a group of distinguished American biologists summed up the principle of cooperation in the statement that the probability of survival of living things increases with the degree in which they harmoniously adjust themselves to each other and to their environment.[117] Today, contrary to the "Nature red in tooth and claw" school of natural selectionists, the evidence increasingly indicates that natural selection favors the cooperative as opposed to the disoperative struggling for survival. We have already quoted Professor Burkholder (page 29) to the effect that "The most important basis for selection is the ability of associated components to work together harmoniously in the organism and among organisms. All new genetic factors, whether they arise from within by mutation or are incorporated from without by various means, are accepted or rejected according to their cooperation with associated components in the whole aggregation." [118]

We begin to understand, then, that the process of evolution is one which favors cooperating rather than disoperating groups, and that "fitness" is a function of the group as a whole rather than of separate individuals. The fitness of the individual is largely derived from his membership in a group. The more cooperative the group, the greater is the fitness for survival which extends to all its members.

Cooperation is the law of life for the group as for the individual. We know that if a child does not receive adequate cooperation—that is to say, an adequate amount of love—from those who raise him, he will not develop into an adequate social being.[119] More than this, we now know that each organism is born with an innate need to be cooperative, to give and receive love, to be good. If the infant's needs are adequately satisfied he cannot help but be good, that is, loving. The biological basis of love, of goodness, consists in the organism's drive to secure cooperation in the satisfaction of its basic needs. It is the satisfactions which the cooperators give it which enables the organism to grow in security. It will readily be understood, therefore, that love is closely allied, if not identical with, cooperation and security.

This realization that the ethical conception of love, at

which almost all peoples have arrived independently, is no mere artificial creation of man, but is firmly grounded in the biological structure of man as a functioning organism, is a discovery of the greatest possible significance for the future of mankind.

To summarize, then, we perceive that the biological basis of cooperation has its origins in the same sources as social behavior, namely, in the process of reproduction; that social, cooperative behavior is but the continuation and development of the maternal-offspring relationship. Cooperative social behavior is therefore as old as life itself, and the course of evolution has, in man, been increasingly directed toward the fuller development of cooperative behavior. Cooperative behavior clearly has great survival value. When social behavior is not cooperative it is disordered behavior. The principle which controls all biologically healthy behavior is love. Love, social behavior, cooperation and security mean very much the same thing. Without love there can be no healthy social behavior, cooperation or security. What men want is to feel related to something, whether to family, friends, or deity. Man does not want independence in the sense of functioning separately from the interests of his fellows. That kind of independence leads to lonesomeness and fear. What man wants is the positive freedom that follows the pattern of his life as an infant within the family—dependent security, the feeling that he is a part of a group, accepted, wanted, loved and loving.

In human beings who develop normally, this feeling of love and unity with the group continues to grow all through life. It is a common observation that the happiest persons are those who most strongly feel a sense of connection with the whole community. They are happiest because they are giving fullest play to their innermost tendencies.[120]

Men who do not love one another are sick—sick not from any disease arising within themselves, but from a disorder which has been encultured within them by the false values of their societies. Belief in false values, in competition instead of cooperation, in class and race and national prejudice instead of cooperation, in narrow selfish interests instead of altruism, in atomism (especially atom-bombism) instead of universalism, in the value of things instead of the value of man, represents man turning upon all that is innately good in him.

Science points the way to survival and happiness for all mankind through love and cooperation. Do what we will, our drives toward goodness are as biologically determined as are our drives toward breathing. Our highly endowed potentialities for social life have been used to pervert and deny their very nature, and this has led us close to the brink of disaster. We cannot continue to deny these potentialities without destroying ourselves.[121]

The findings of contemporary science in this field are fraught with meaning of the greatest significance for mankind. They give support to all forces that are attempting to weld men closer together, and so to improve the quality and increase the quantity of security for all individuals. These findings turn the weight of science against all advocates of separatism, isolationism, aggressive individualism. It brands the theories of the race discriminators, the hate-mongers, not merely as immoral but as unnatural. These findings give greater support than ever to Darwin's conclusion that "As man advances in civilization, and small tribes are united into larger communities, the simplest reason would tell each individual that he ought to extend his social instincts and sympathies to all members of the same nation, though personally unknown to him. This point being once reached, there is only an artificial barrier to prevent his sympathies extending to the men of all nations and races." [122]

Man is bound to his fellow men by an unbreakable bond—by life itself.

The UNESCO Statement on Race concludes with a thought taken from a sermon by the English divine and poet John Donne (1572?-1631). We could not more appropriately conclude this work than in the words of John Donne:

> No man is an *Island*, entire of itself; every man
> is a piece of the *Continent*, a part of the *main*;
> if a *Clod* be washed away by the *Sea*, *Europe* is the
> less, as well as if a *Promontory* were, as well as if
> a *Manor* of thy *friends* or of thine own were; any
> man's *death* diminishes *me*, because I am involved
> in *Mankind*; And therefore never send to know for
> whom the *bell* tolls; it tolls for thee. [123]

Introduction to the Second UNESCO Statement on Race

Following the publication of the first Statement On Race a number of scientists felt that they could not agree with everything in it. It was also felt that there had not been a sufficient representation of physical anthropologists and geneticists on the first Committee, even though the early drafts of the first Statement had been circulated among such scientists for comment and criticism. It was, therefore, decided to call together a second Committee comprised of representative physical anthropologists and geneticists. This Committee met at the Paris headquarters of UNESCO from the 4th to the 8th of June 1951. The seven physical anthropologists and five geneticists comprising the second Committee agreed that the best procedure would be to go over every word of the first Statement and use the revision as the basis for the second Statement. The resulting discussions were fascinating, and the "Statement on the Nature of Race and Race Differences" issued in September 1951, reflects something of the nature of those discussions, so ably summarized by the rapporteur, Professor L. C. Dunn in his prefatory remarks to this second Statement.

The members of the second Committee were:
Professor R. A. M. Bergman, Royal Tropical Institute, Amsterdam

Professor Gunnar Dahlberg, Director, State Institute for Human Genetics and Race Biology, University of Uppsala

Professor L. C. Dunn, Department of Zoology, Columbia University, New York

Professor J. B. S. Haldane, Head, Department of Biometry, University College, London

Professor Ashley Montagu, Chairman, Department of Anthropology, Rutgers University, New Brunswick, N.J.

Dr. A. E. Mourant, Director, Blood Group Reference Laboratory, Lister Institute, London

Professor Hans Nachtsheim, Director, Institut für Genetik, Freie Universität, Berlin

Dr. Eugène Schreider, Directeur adjoint du Laboratoire d'Anthropologie Physique de l'Ecole des Hautes Etudes, Paris

Dr. Harry L. Shapiro, Chairman, Department of Anthropology, American Museum of Natural History, New York

Dr. J. C. Trevor, Faculty of Archaeology and Anthropology, University of Cambridge

Dr. Henri V. Vallois, Professeur au Musée d'Histoire Naturelle, Directeur du Musée de l'Homme, Paris

Professor S. Zuckerman, Head, Department of Anatomy, Medical School, University of Birmingham

In addition, Dr. Julian Huxley, and Professor T. Dobzhansky, the latter Professor of Zoology, Columbia University, New York, contributed to the final wording.

Comparison between the first and the second Statements will show that there is, in fact, very little difference between them. But while this second Statement expresses the views of physical anthropologists and gneticists, it is to be noted that both Statements are in substantial agreement. Thus, the students of man as a social creature whose behavior varies with every culture, and the students of man's genetic development, his likenesses and differences, are in essential agreement as to the meaning of those likenesses and differences. The second Statement, therefore, requires no annotation—it is self-explanatory particularly when viewed in the light of the annotations to the first Statement.

Statement on the nature of race and race differences

PARIS, June 1951

The reasons for convening a second meeting of experts to discuss the concept of race were chiefly these:

Race is a question of interest to many different kinds of people, not only to the public at large, but to sociologists, anthropologists and biologists, especially those dealing with problems of genetics. At the first discussion on the problem of race, it was chiefly sociologists who gave their opinions and framed the 'Statement on race'. That statement had a good effect, but it did not carry the authority of just those groups within whose special province fall the biological problems of race, namely the physical anthropologists and geneticists. Secondly, the first statement did not, in all its details, carry conviction of these groups and, because of this, it was not supported by many authorities in these two fields.

In general, the chief conclusions of the first statement were sustained, but with differences in emphasis and with some important deletions.

There was no delay or hesitation or lack of unanimity in reaching the primary conclusion that there were no scientific grounds whatever for the racialist position regarding purity of race and the hierarchy of inferior and superior races to which this leads.

We agreed that all races were mixed and that intraracial variability in most biological characters was as great as, if not greater than, interracial variability.

We agreed that races had reached their present states by the operation of evolutionary factors by which different proportions of similar hereditary elements (genes) had become characteristic of different, partially separated groups. The source of these elements seemed to all of us to be the variability which arises by random mutation, and the isolating factors bringing about racial differentiation by preventing intermingling of groups with different mutations, chiefly geographical for the main groups such as African, European and Asiatic.

Man, we recognized, is distinguished as much by his culture as by his biology, and it was clear to all of us that many of the factors leading to the formation of minor races of men have been cultural. Anything that tends to prevent free exchange of genes amongst groups is a potential race-making factor and these partial barriers may be religious, social and linguistic, as well as geographical.

We were careful to avoid dogmatic definitions of race, since, as a product of evolutionary factors, it is a dynamic rather than a static concept. We were equally careful to avoid saying that, because races were all variable and many of them graded into each other, therefore races did not exist. The physical anthropologists and the man in the street both know that races exist; the former, from the scientifically recognizable and measurable congeries of traits which he uses in classifying the varieties of man; the latter from the immediate evidence of his senses when he sees an African, a European, an Asiatic and an American Indian together.

We had no difficulty in agreeing that no evidence of differences in innate mental ability between different racial groups has been adduced, but that here too intraracial variability is at least as great as interracial variability. We agreed that psychological traits could not be used in classifying races, nor could they serve as parts of racial descriptions.

We were fortunate in having as members of our conference several scientists who had made special studies of the results of intermarriage between members of different races. This meant that our conclusion that race mixture in general did not lead to disadvantageous results was based on actual experience as well as upon study of the literature. Many of our members thought it quite likely that hydridization of different races could lead to biologically advantageous results, although there was insufficient evidence to support any conclusion.

Since race, as a word, has become coloured by its misuse in connexion with national, linguistic and religious differences, and by its deliberate abuse by racialists, we tried to find a new word to express the same meaning of a biologically differentiated group. On this we did not succeed, but agreed to reserve race as the word to be used for anthropological classification of groups showing definite combinations of physical (including physiological) traits in characteristic proportions.

We also tried hard, but again we failed, to reach some general statement about the inborn nature of man with respect to his behaviour toward his fellows. It is obvious that members of a group show co-operative or associative behaviour towards each other, while members of different groups may show aggressive behaviour towards each other and both of these attitudes may occur within the same individual. We recognized that the understanding of the psychological origin of race prejudice was an important problem which called for further study.

Nevertheless, having regard to the limitations of our present knowledge, all of us believed that the biological differences found amongst human racial groups can in no case justify the views of racial inequality which have been based on ignorance and prejudice, and that all of the differences which we know can well be disregarded for all ethical human purposes.

L. C. DUNN (rapporteur),
June 1951

1. Scientists are generally agreed that all men living today belong to a single species, *Homo sapiens,* and are derived from a common stock, even though there is some dispute as to when and how different human groups diverged from this common stock.

The concept of race is unanimously regarded by anthropologists as a classificatory device providing a zoological frame within which the various groups of mankind may be arranged and by means of which studies of evolutionary processes can be facilitated. In its anthropological sense, the word "race" should be reserved for groups of mankind possessing well-developed and primarily heritable physical differences from other groups. Many populations can be so classified but, because of the complexity of human history, there are also many populations which cannot easily be fitted into a racial classification.

2. Some of the physical differences between human groups are due to differences in hereditary constitution and some to differences in the environments in which they have been brought up. In most cases, both influences have been at work. The science of genetics suggests that the hereditary differences among populations of a single species are the results of the action of two sets of processes. On the one hand, the genetic composition of isolated populations is constantly but gradually being altered by natural selection and by occasional changes (mutations) in the material particles (genes) which control heredity. Populations are also affected by fortuitous changes in gene frequency and by marriage customs. On the other hand, crossing is constantly breaking down the differentiations so set up. The new mixed populations, in so far as they, in turn, become isolated, are subject to the same processes, and these may lead to further changes. Existing races are merely the result, considered at a particular moment in time, of the total effect of such processes on the human species. The hereditary characters to be used in the classification of human groups, the limits

of their variation within these groups, and thus the extent of
the classificatory sub-divisions adopted may legitimately differ
according to the scientific purpose in view.

3. National, religious, geographical, linguistic and cultural
groups do not necessarily coincide with racial groups; and the
cultural traits of such groups have no demonstrated connexion
with racial traits. Americans are not a race, nor are Frenchmen, nor Germans; nor *ipso facto* is any other national group.
Moslems and Jews are no more races than are Roman Catholics
and Protestants; nor are people who live in Iceland or Britain
or India, or who speak English or any other language, or who
are culturally Turkish or Chinese and the like, thereby describable as races. The use of the term "race" in speaking of such
groups may be a serious error, but it is one which is habitually
committed.

4. Human races can be, and have been, classified in different
ways by different anthropologists. Most of them agree in classifying the greater part of existing mankind into at least three
large units, which may be called major groups (in French
grand-races, in German *Hauptrassen*). Such a classification does
not depend on any single physical character, nor does for example, skin colour by itself necessarily distinguish one major
group from another. Furthermore, so far as it has been possible
to analyse them, the differences in physical structure which distinguish one major group from another give no support to
popular notions of any general "superiority" or "inferiority"
which are sometimes implied in referring to these groups.

Broadly speaking, individuals belonging to different major
groups of mankind are distinguishable by virtue of their physical characters, but individual members, or small groups belonging to different races within the same major group are usually
not so distinguishable. Even the major groups grade into each
other, and the physical traits by which they and the races
within them are characterized overlap considerably. With respect to most, if not all, measurable characters, the differences
among individuals belonging to the same race are greater than

the differences that occur between the observed averages for two or more races within the same major group.

5. Most anthropologists do not include mental characteristics in their classification of human races. Studies within a single race have shown that both innate capacity and environmental opportunity determine the results of tests of intelligence and temperament, though their relative importance is disputed.

When intelligence tests, even non-verbal, are made on a group of non-literate people, their scores are usually lower than those of more civilized people. It has been recorded that different groups of the same race occupying similarly high levels of civilization may yield considerable differences in intelligence tests. When, however, the two groups have been brought up from childhood in similar environments, the differences are usually very slight. Moreover, there is good evidence that, given similar opportunities, the average performance (that is to say, the performance of the individual who is representative because he is surpassed by as many as he surpasses), and the variation round it, do not differ appreciably from one race to another.

Even those psychologists who claim to have found the greatest differences in intelligence between groups of different racial origin and have contended that they are hereditary, always report that some members of the group of inferior performance surpass not merely the lowest ranking member of the superior group but also the average of its members. In any case, it has never been possible to separate members of two groups on the basis of mental capacity, as they can often be separated on a basis of religion, skin colour, hair form or language. It is possible, though not proved, that some types of innate capacity for intellectual and emotional responses are commoner in one human group than in another, but it is certain that, within a single group, innate capacities vary as much as, if not more than, they do between different groups.

The study of the heredity of psychological characteristics is beset with difficulties. We know that certain mental diseases and defects are transmitted from one generation to the next, but we are less familiar with the part played by heredity in the mental life of normal individuals. The normal individual, irrespective of race, is essentially educable. It follows that his intellectual and moral life is largely conditioned by his training and by his physical and social environment.

It often happens that a national group may appear to be characterized by particular psychological attributes. The superficial view would be that this is due to race. Scientifically, however, we realize that any common psychological attribute is more likely to be due to a common historical and social background, and that such attributes may obscure the fact that, within different populations consisting of many human types, one will find approximately the same range of temperament and intelligence.

6. The scientific material available to us at present does not justify the conclusion that inherited genetic differences are a major factor in producing the differences between the cultures and cultural achievements of different peoples or groups. It does indicate, on the contrary, that a major factor in explaining such differences is the cultural experience which each group has undergone.

7. There is no evidence for the existence of so-called "pure" races. Skeletal remains provide the basis of our limited knowledge about earlier races. In regard to race mixture, the evidence points to the fact that human hybridization has been going on for an indefinite but considerable time. Indeed, one of the processes of race formation and race extinction or absorption is by means of hybridization between races. As there is no reliable evidence that disadvantageous effects are produced thereby, no biological justification exists for prohibiting intermarriage between persons of different races.

8. We now have to consider the bearing of these statements on the problem of human equality. We wish to emphasize that equality of opportunity and equality in law in no way depend,

as ethical principles, upon the assertion that human beings are in fact equal in endowment.

9. We have thought it worth while to set out in a formal manner what is at present scientifically established concerning individual and group differences:

(a) In matters of race, the only characteristics which anthropologists have so far been able to use effectively as a basis for classification are physical (anatomical and physiological).

(b) Available scientific knowledge provides no basis for believing that the groups of mankind differ in their innate capacity for intellectual and emotional development.

(c) Some biological differences between human beings within a single race may be as great as, or greater than, the same biological differences between races.

(d) Vast social changes have occurred that have not been connected in any way with changes in racial type. Historical and sociological studies thus support the view that genetic differences are of little significance in determining the social and cultural differences between different groups of men.

(e) There is no evidence that race mixture produces disadvantageous results from a biological point of view. The social results of race mixture, whether for good or ill, can generally be traced to social factors.

Text drafted at Unesco House, Paris, on 8 June 1951, by:

Professor R. A. M. Borgman, Royal Tropical Institute, Amsterdam;

Professor Gunnar Dahlberg, Director, State Institute for Human Genetics and Race Biology, University of Uppsala;

Professor L. C. Dunn, Department of Zoology, Columbia University, New York;

Professor J. B. S. Haldane, Head, Department of Biometry, University College, London;

Professor M. F. Ashley Montagu, Chairman, Department of Anthropology, Rutgers University, New Brunswick, N.J.;

Dr. A. E. Mourant, Director, Blood Group Reference Laboratory, Lister Institute, London;

Professor Hans Nachtscheim, Director, Institut für Genetik, Freie Universität, Berlin;

Dr. Eugène Schreider, Directeur adjoint du Laboratoire d'Anthropologie Physique de l'Ecole des Hautes Etudes, Paris;

Professor Harry L. Shapiro, Chairman, Department of Anthropology, American Museum of Natural History, New York;

Dr. J. C. Trevor, Faculty of Archaeology and Anthropology, University of Cambridge;

Dr. Henri V. Vallois, Professeur au Musée d'Histoire Naturelle, Directeur du Musée de l'Homme, Paris;

Professor S. Zuckerman, Head, Department of Anatomy, Medical School, University of Birmingham;

Professor Th. Dobzhansky, Department of Zoology, Columbia University, New York;

Dr. Julian Huxley contributed to the final wording.

The Third UNESCO Statement on Race

The Third Unesco Statement on Race was drawn up at Moscow, U.S.S.R., on 18 August 1964. Its primary purpose was to re-examine the biological aspects of the Statements on Race and Racial Differences issued in 1950 and 1951, and to provide the biological foundations for a further Statement to be published in 1966. The projected Statement was actually published in 1967 (see pp. 157-64).

The third Statement presents an admirably clear exposition of the facts relating to the biology of race. It speaks eloquently for itself, and requires no further exposition here.

III

Proposals on the biological aspects of race

MOSCOW, August 1964

The undersigned, assembled by UNESCO in order to give their views on the biological aspects of the race question and in particular to formulate the biological part for a statement foreseen for 1966 and intended to bring up to date and to complete the declaration on the nature of race and racial differences signed in 1951, have unanimously agreed on the following:

1. All men living today belong to a single species, *Homo sapiens,* and are derived from a common stock. There are differences of opinion regarding how and when different human groups diverged from this common stock.

2. Biological differences between human beings are due to

differences in hereditary constitution and to the influence of
the environment on this genetic potential. In most cases, those
differences are due to the interaction of these two sets of
factors.

3. There is great genetic diversity within all human populations. Pure races—in the sense of genetically homogeneous
populations—do not exist in the human species.

4. There are obvious physical differences between populations living in different geographical areas of the world, in
their average appearance. Many of these differences have a genetic component.

Most often the latter consist in differences in the frequency
of the same hereditary characters.

5. Different classifications of mankind into major stocks, and
of those into more restricted categories (races, which are groups
of populations, or single populations) have been proposed on
the basis of hereditary physical traits. Nearly all classifications
recognize at least three major stocks.

Since the pattern of geographic variation of the characteristics used in racial classification is a complex one, and since
this pattern does not present any major discontinuity, these
classifications, whatever they are, cannot claim to classify mankind into clearcut categories; moreover, on account of the com-
plexities of human history, it is difficult to determine the place
of certain groups within these racial classifications, in particular that of certain intermediate populations.

Many anthropologists, while stressing the importance of human variation, believe that the scientific interest of these classifications is limited, and even that they carry the risk of inviting
abusive generalizations.

Differences between individuals within a race or within a
population are often greater than the average differences between races or populations.

Some of the variable distinctive traits which are generally
chosen as criteria to characterize a race are either independently inherited or show only varying degrees of association be-

tween them within each population. Therefore, the combination of these traits in most individuals does not correspond to the typological racial characterization.

6. In man as well as in animals, the genetic composition of each population is subject to the modifying influence of diverse factors: natural selection, tending towards adaptation to the environment, fortuitous mutations which lead to modifications of the molecules of deoxyribonucleic acid which determine heredity, or random modifications in the frequency of qualitative hereditary characters, to an extent dependent on the patterns of mating and the size of populations.

Certain physical characters have a universal biological value for the survival of the human species, irrespective of the environment. The differences on which racial classifications are based do not affect these characters, and therefore, it is not possible from the biological point of view to speak in any way whatsoever of a general inferiority or superiority of this or that race.

7. Human evolution presents attributes of capital importance which are specific to the species.

The human species which is now spread over the whole world, has a past rich in migrations, in territorial expansions and contractions.

As a consequence, general adaptability to the most diverse environments is in man more pronounced than his adaptation to specific environments.

For long millenniums progress made by man, in any field, seems to have been increasingly, if not exclusively, based on culture and the transmission of cultural achievements and not on the transmission of genetic endowment. This implies a modification in the role of natural selection in man today.

On account of the mobility of human populations and of social factors, mating between members of different human groups which tend to mitigate the differentiations acquired, has played a much more important role in human history than in that of animals. The history of any human population or of any human race, is rich in instances of hybridization and those tend to become more and more numerous.

For man, the obstacles to interbreeding are geographical as well as social and cultural.

8. At all times, the hereditary characteristics of the human populations are in dynamic equilibrium as a result of this interbreeding and of the differentiation mechanisms which were mentioned before. As entities defined by sets of distinctive traits, human races are at any time in a process of emergence and dissolution.

Human races in general present a far less clearcut characterization than many animal races and they cannot be compared at all to races of domestic animals, these being the result of heightened selection for special purposes.

9. It has never been proved that interbreeding has biological disadvantages for mankind as a whole.

On the contrary, it contributes to the maintenance of biological ties between human groups and thus to the unity of the species in its diversity.

The biological consequences of a marriage depend only on the individual genetic make-up of the couple and not on their race.

Therefore, no biological justification exists for prohibiting intermarriage between persons of different races, or for advising against it on racial grounds.

10. Man since his origin has at his disposal ever more efficient cultural means of nongenetic adaptation.

11. Those cultural factors which break social and geographic barriers, enlarge the size of the breeding populations and so act upon their genetic structure by diminishing the random fluctuations (genetic drift).

12. As a rule, the major stocks extend over vast territories encompassing many diverse populations which differ in language, economy, culture, etc.

There is no national, religious, geographic, linguistic, or cultural group which constitutes a race *ipso facto*; the concept of race is purely biological.

However, human beings who speak the same language and share the same culture have a tendency to intermarry, and often there is as a result a certain degree of coincidence between physical traits on the one hand, and linguistic and cultural traits on the other. But there is no known causal nexus between these and therefore it is not justifiable to attribute cultural characteristics to the influence of the genetic inheritance.

13. Most racial classifications of mankind do not include mental traits or attributes as a taxonomic criterion.

Heredity may have an influence in the variability shown by individuals within a given population in their responses to the psychological tests currently applied.

However, no difference has ever been detected convincingly in the hereditary endowments of human groups in regard to what is measured by these tests. On the other hand, ample evidence attests to the influence of physical, cultural and social environment on differences in response to these tests.

The study of this question is hampered by the very great difficulty of determining what part heredity plays in the average differences observed in so-called tests of over-all intelligence between populations of different cultures.

The genetic capacity for intellectual development, like certain major anatomical traits peculiar to the species, is one of the biological traits essential for its survival in any natural or social environment.

The peoples of the world today appear to possess equal biological potentialities for attaining any civilizational level. Differences in the achievements of different peoples must be attributed solely to their cultural history.

Certain psychological traits are at times attributed to particular peoples. Whether or not such assertions are valid, we do not find any basis for ascribing such traits to hereditary factors, until proof to the contrary is given.

Neither in the field of hereditary potentialities concerning the overall intelligence and the capacity for cultural development, nor in that of physical traits, is there any justification for the concept of 'inferior' and 'superior' races.

The biological data given above stand in open contradiction to the tenets of racism. Racist theories can in no way pretend to have any scientific foundation and the anthropologists should endeavour to prevent the results of their researches from being used in such a biased way that they would serve non-scientific ends.

Moscow, 18 August 1964.

Professor Nigel Barnicot, Department of Anthropology, University College, London;

Professor Jean Benoist, Director, Department of Anthropology, University of Montreal, Montreal;

Professor Tadeusz Bielicki, Institute of Anthropology, Polish Academy of Sciences, Wroclaw;

Dr. A. E. Boyo, Head, Federal Malaria Research Institute, Department of Pathology and Haematology, Lagos University Medical School, Lagos;

Professor V. V. Bunak, Institute of Ethnography, Moscow;

Professor Carleton S. Coon, Curator, The University Museum, University of Pennsylvania, Philadelphia, Pa. (United States);

Professor G. F. Debetz, Institute of Ethnography, Moscow;

Mrs. Adelaide G. de Diaz Ungria, Curator, Museum of Natural Sciences, Caracas;

Professor Santiago Genoves, Institute of Historical Research, Faculty of Sciences, University of Mexico, Mexico;

Professor Robert Gessain, Director, Centre of Anthropological Research, Musée de l'Homme, Paris;

Professor Jean Hiernaux, (Scientific Director of the meeting), Laboratory of Anthropology, Faculty of Sciences, University of Paris, Institute of Sociology, Free University of Brussels;

Dr. *Yaya Kane, Director, Senegal National Centre of Blood Transfusion, Dakar;*

Professor *Ramakhrishna Mukherjee, Head, Sociological Research Unit, Indian Statistical Institute, Calcutta;*

Professor *Bernard Rensch, Zoological Institute, Westfälische Wilhelms-Universität, Münster (Federal Republic of Germany);*

Professor *Y. Y. Roguinski, Institute of Ethnography, Moscow;*

Professor *Francisco M. Salzano, Institute of Natural Sciences, Pôrto Alegre, Rio Grande do Sul (Brazil);*

Professor *Alf Sommerfelt, Rector, Oslo University, Oslo;*

Professor *James N. Spuhler, Department of Anthropology, University of Michigan, Ann Arbor, Mich. (United States);*

Professor *Hisashi Suzuki, Department of Anthropology, Faculty of Science, University of Tokyo, Tokyo;*

Professor *J. A. Valsik, Department of Anthropology and Genetics, J. A. Komensky University, Bratislava (Czechoslovakia);*

Dr. *Joseph S. Weiner, London School of Hygiene and Tropical Medicine, University of London, London;*

Professor *V. P. Yakimov, Moscow State University, Institute of Anthropology, Moscow.*

The Fourth UNESCO Statement on Race

The Fourth UNESCO Statement on Race was drafted at the meetings held at Unesco House in Paris, 18 to 26 September 1967. This fourth Statement differs from those preceding it in that its emphasis is almost entirely on the historical, social, and political causes of racism, and in that it makes specific recommendations for social and political action in order to combat racism more effectively. Because of the social and political considerations involved, this fourth Statement will be followed by an extended commentary and discussion.

IV

Statement on race and racial prejudice

1. "All men are born free and equal both in dignity and in rights." This universally proclaimed democratic principle stands in jeopardy wherever political, economic, social and cultural inequalities affect human group relations. A particularly striking obstacle to the recognition of equal dignity for all is racism. Racism continues to haunt the world. As a major social phenomenon it requires the attention of all students of the sciences of man.

2. Racism stultifies the development of those who suffer from it, perverts those who apply it, divides nations within themselves, aggravates international conflict and threatens world peace.

3. Conference of experts meeting in Paris in September 1967, agreed that racist doctrines lack any scientific basis whatsoever. It reaffirmed the propositions adopted by the international meeting held in Moscow in 1964 which was called to re-examine the biological aspects of the statements on race and racial differences issued in 1950 and 1951. In particular, it draws attention to the following points:

(a) All men living today belong to the same species and descend from the same stock.

(b) The division of the human species into "races" is partly conventional and partly arbitrary and does not imply any hierarchy whatsoever. Many anthropologists stress the importance of human variation, but believe that "racial" divisions have limited scientific interest and may even carry the risk of inviting abusive generalization.

(c) Current biological knowledge does not permit us to impute cultural achievements to differences in genetic potential. Differences in the achievements of different peoples should be attributed solely to their cultural history. The peoples of the world today appear to possess equal biological potentialities for attaining any level of civilization.

Racism grossly falsifies the knowledge of human biology.

4. The human problems arising from so-called "race" relations are social in origin rather than biological. A basic problem is racism, namely, antisocial beliefs and acts which are based on the fallacy that discriminatory intergroup relations are justifiable on biological grounds.

5. Groups commonly evaluate their characteristics in comparison with others. Racism falsely claims that there is a scientific basis for arranging groups hierarchically in terms of psychological and cultural characteristics that are immutable and innate. In this way it seeks to make existing differences appear inviolable as a means of permanently maintaining current relations between groups.

6. Faced with the exposure of the falsity of its biological doc-

trines, racism finds ever new stratagems for justifying the inequality of groups. It points to the fact that groups do not intermarry, a fact which follows, in part, from the divisions created by racism. It uses this fact to argue the thesis that this absence of intermarriage derives from differences of a biological order. Whenever it fails in its attempts to prove that the source of group differences lies in the biological field, it falls backs upon justifications in terms of divine purpose, cultural differences, disparity of educational standards or some other doctrine which would serve to mask its continued racist beliefs. Thus, many of the problems which racism presents in the world today do not arise merely from its open manifestations, but from the activities of those who discriminate on racial grounds but are unwilling to acknowledge it.

7. Racism has historical roots. It has not been a universal phenomenon. Many contemporary societies and cultures show little trace of it. It was not evident for long periods in world history. Many forms of racism have arisen out of the conditions of conquest, out of the justification of Negro slavery and its aftermath of racial inequality in the West, and out of the colonial relationship. Among other examples is that of antisemitism, which has played a particular role in history, with Jews being the chosen scapegoat to take the blame for problems and crises met by many societies.

8. The anti-colonial revolution of the twentieth century has opened up new possibilities for eliminating the scourge of racism. In some formerly dependent countries, people formerly classified as inferior have for the first time obtained full political rights. Moreover, the participation of formerly dependent nations in international organizations in terms of equality has done much to undermine racism.

9. There are, however, some instances in certain societies in which groups, victims of racialistic practices, have themselves applied doctrines with racist implications in their struggle for freedom. Such an attitude is a secondary phenomenon, a reaction stemming from men's search for an identity which prior

racist theory and racialistic practices denied them. None the less, the new forms of racist ideology, resulting from this prior exploitation, have no justification in biology. They are a product of a political struggle and have no scientific foundation.

10. In order to undermine racism it is not sufficient that biologists should expose its fallacies. It is also necessary that psychologists and sociologists should demonstrate its causes. The social structure is always an important factor. However, within the same social structure, there may be great individual variation in racialistic behaviour, associated with the personality of the individuals and their personal circumstances.

11. The committee of experts agreed on the following conclusions about the social causes of race prejudice:

(a) Social and economic causes of racial prejudice are particularly observed in settler societies wherein are found conditions of great disparity of power and property, in certain urban areas where there have emerged ghettoes in which individuals are deprived of equal access to employment, housing, political participation, education, and the administration of justice, and in many societies where social and economic tasks which are deemed to be contrary to the ethics or beneath the dignity of its members are assigned to a group of different origins who are derided, blamed, and punished for taking on these tasks.

(b) Individuals with certain personality troubles may be particularly inclined to adopt and manifest racial prejudices. Small groups, associations, and social movements of a certain kind sometimes preserve and transmit racial prejudices. The foundations of the prejudices lie, however, in the economic and social system of a society.

(c) Racism tends to be cumulative. Discrimination deprives a group of equal treatment and presents that group as a problem. The group then tends to be blamed for its own condition, leading to further elaboration of racist theory.

12. The major techniques for coping with racism involve changing those social situations which give rise to prejudice,

preventing the prejudiced from acting in accordance with their beliefs, and combating the false beliefs themselves.

13. It is recognized that the basically important changes in the social structure that may lead to the elimination of racial prejudice may require decisions of a political nature. It is also recognized, however, that certain agencies of enlightenment, such as education and other means of social and economic advancement, mass media, and law can be immediately and effectively mobilized for the elimination of racial prejudice.

14. The school and other instruments for social and economic progress can be one of the most effective agents for the achievement of broadened understanding and the fulfilment of the potentialities of man. They can equally much be used for the perpetuation of discrimination and inequality. It is therefore essential that the resources for education and for social and economic action of all nations be employed in two ways:

(a) The schools should ensure that their curricula contain scientific understandings about race and human unity, and that invidious distinctions about peoples are not made in texts and classrooms.

(b) (i) Because the skills to be gained in formal and vocational education become increasingly important with the processes of technological development, the resources of the schools and other resources should be fully available to all parts of the population with neither restriction nor discrimination;

(ii) Furthermore, in cases where, for historical reasons, certain groups have a lower average education and economic standing, it is the responsibility of the society to take corrective measures. These measures should ensure, so far as possible, that the limitations of poor environments are not passed on to the children.

In view of the importance of teachers in any educational programme, special attention should be given to their training.

Teachers should be made conscious of the degree to which they reflect the prejudices which may be current in their society. They should be encouraged to avoid these prejudices.

15. Governmental units and other organizations concerned should give special attention to improving the housing situations and work opportunities available to victims of racism. This will not only counteract the effects of racism, but in itself can be a positive way of modifying racist attitudes and behaviour.

16. The media of mass communication are increasingly important in promoting knowledge and understanding, but their exact potentiality is not fully known. Continuing research into the social utilization of the media is needed in order to assess their influence in relation to formation of attitudes and behavioural patterns in the field of race prejudice and race discrimination. Because the mass media reach vast numbers of people at different educational and social levels, their role in encouraging or combating race prejudice can be crucial. Those who work in these media should maintain a positive approach to the promotion of understanding between groups and populations. Representation of peoples in stereotypes and holding them up to ridicule should be avoided. Attachment to news reports of racial designations which are not germane to the accounts should also be avoided.

17. Law is among the most important means of ensuring equality between individuals and one of the most effective means of fighting racism.

The Universal Declaration of Human Rights of 10 December 1948 and the related international agreements and conventions which have taken effect subsequently can contribute effectively, on both the national and international level, to the fight against any injustice of racist origin.

National legislation is a means of effectively outlawing racist propaganda and acts based upon racial discrimination. Moreover, the policy expressed in such legislation must bind not only the courts and judges charged with its enforcement, but also all agencies of government of whatever level or whatever character.

It is not claimed that legislation can immediately eliminate prejudice. Nevertheless, by being a means of protecting the victims of acts based upon prejudice, and by setting a moral example backed by the dignity of the courts, it can, in the long run, even change attitudes.

18. Ethnic groups which represent the object of some form of discrimination are sometimes accepted and tolerated by dominating groups at the cost of their having to abandon completely their cultural identity. It should be stressed that the effort of these ethnic groups to preserve their cultural values should be encouraged. They will thus be better able to contribute to the enrichment of the total culture of humanity.

19. Racial prejudice and discrimination in the world today arise from historical and social phenomena and falsely claim the sanction of science. It is, therefore, the responsibility of all biological and social scientists, philosophers, and others working in related disciplines, to ensure that the results of their research are not misused by those who wish to propagate racial prejudice and encourage discrimination.

This statement was prepared by a committee of experts on race and racial prejudice which met at Unesco House, Paris, from 18 to 26 September 1967. The following experts took part in the committee's work:

Professor Muddathir Abdel Rahim, University of Khartoum (Sudan);

Professor Georges Balandier, Université de Paris (France);

Professor Celio de Oliveira Borja, University of Guanabara (Brazil);

Professor Lloyd Braithwaite, University of the West Indies (Jamaica);

Professor Leonard Broom, University of Texas (United States);

Professor G. F. Debetz, Institute of Ethnography, Moscow (U.S.S.R.);

Professor J. Djordjevic, University of Belgrade (Yugoslavia);
Dean Clarence Clyde Ferguson, Howard University (United States);
Dr. Dharam P. Ghai, University College (Kenya);
Professor Louis Guttman, Hebrew University (Israel);
Professor Jean Hiernaux, Université Libre de Bruxelles (Belgium);
Professor A. Kloskowska, University of Lodz (Poland);
Judge Kéba M'Baye, President of the Supreme Court (Senegal);
Professor John Rex, University of Durham (United Kingdom);
Professor Mariano R. Solveira, University of Havana (Cuba);
Professor Hisashi Suzuki, University of Tokyo (Japan)
Dr. Romila Thapar, University of Delhi (India);
Professor C. H. Waddington, University of Edinburgh (United Kingdom).

PARAGRAPH 1

"All men are born free and equal both in dignity and in rights." This universally proclaimed democratic principle stands in jeopardy wherever political, economic, social and cultural inequalities affect human group relations. A particularly striking obstacle to the recognition of equal dignity for all is racism. Racism continues to haunt the world. As a major social phenomenon it requires the attention of all students of the sciences of man.

If there has been one principal point that has been emphasized in the first and in all the subsequent statements on race it has been that by virtue of the fact that every individual is a human being within the brotherhood of man his birthright is development and fulfillment of himself. That by virtue of the fact that he is a human being he is entitled to all the rights and privileges of humanity. Furthermore, that anyone who places the least impediment in the way of any human being's development or fulfillment, commits the greatest of all offenses against the human spirit, since the most valuable treasure of humanity lies in the wealth of human uniqueness which each individual has to contribute to the common wealth of humanity. It is for this reason a crime, not alone against the individual, but against humanity, to deprive any person of the opportunity to fulfill himself to the optimum. It is because racism does just this that it must be considered as the most destructive of all the sins against the human spirit and as the most self-corrosive of anti-human doctrines, for any man who keeps another down in the mud cannot be anything but muddied himself.

The question at issue is a very simple one. It is this: is this person a human being? If the answer is that he is, then it should follow that he is entitled to all the rights and privileges and obligations of humanity. And this is an ethical principle. It has nothing whatever to do with the findings of science. It is not a scientific question. It is a matter of ethics, of morality. And that is the long and short of it.

And this brings us to the real question: shall we by statements and by discussions on race ever solve the problem of racism? It is doubtful. At best we may succeed in reducing the virulence of the disease by making clear the nature of the pathogenic ideas that make it possible. Where the various Statements could have been improved, I think, would have been in offering some discussion of the political, social, religious, and economic forces that play so important a role in the genesis and maintenance of racism. Above all, we must understand that the ethical questions involved in human relations imply that there can be no real solution to the problem of racism until people become humane beings. So that it must be the teaching of potential humane beings how to become so that must be our primary task, if the problem of racism, as well as many other human problems is to be solved.[124] Human society is sustained by the sense of human dignity, the respect that man gives to man. It falls apart into anarchies of power, fear, and conflict when its conception of humanity is degraded and falsified.

This paragraph most explicitly means what it says. It does not mean anything so fatuous as that all men are born biologically equal. The variability in the human species, especially in the capacity for behavior as between one individual and another, is enormous. It is ridiculous to claim that all human beings have the same capacities for behavioral achievement. There is great variability in every group for every sort of behavioral capacity. It is this diversity in likeness that constitutes the riches of mankind.

PARAGRAPH 2

R acism stultifies the development of those who suffer from it, perverts those who apply it, divides nations within themselves, aggravates international conflict and threatens world peace.

B ecause racism cuts off human beings from the natural enrichments which each has to offer to the other, everyone is impoverished. Racism, by the narrow view it takes of other human beings, has the effect of narrowing the vision and making bigots of those who practise it. A bigot, said Oliver Wendell Holmes, is like the pupil of the eye, the more light you expose it to the narrower it grows. The racist becomes arrested at a level of development at which emotion does service for intelligence, and anger, fear, and anxiety do service for amity, security, involvement, and respect for others. Racism is reductionist, and he who reduces another man reduces himself, for the essence and meaning of humanity is involvement in the welfare of *all* other human beings. No human being can be considered of less worth in the scale of humanity than any other. This does not mean that all human beings are endowed with equal potentialities for achievement in the intellectual or any other world—they are not. What a bore it would be if all human beings were alike in their capacities. What the statement that all human beings are of equal worth means is that their humanity is of equal worth, that every human being is born with equal rights to his humanity, the right to the development of his humanity and his potentialities, however unbounded or limited they may be.

When we help others to develop, we develop ourselves. When we deprive others, we deprive ourselves.

Wherever racism flourishes, as in South Africa and the United States, the divisions, conflicts, social breakdown, and disorganization are so costly and so threatening that the very continuation of such societies is in constant jeopardy. The racist policies of many nations, especially against Blacks, also threaten world peace, by creating bad feeling between Black and White peoples.[125]

PARAGRAPH 3

Conference of experts meeting in Paris in September
1967, agreed that racist doctrines lack any scientific
basis whatsoever. It reaffirmed the proposition adopted by
the international meeting held in Moscow in 1964 which
was called to re-examine the biological aspects of the statements on race and racial differences issued in 1950 and
1951. In particular, it draws attention to the following
points:

    (a) *All men living today belong to the same species and
        descend from the same stock.*

    (b) *The division of the human species into "races" is
        partly conventional and partly arbitrary and does
        not imply any hierarchy whatsoever. Many anthro-
        pologists stress the importance of human variation,
        but believe that "racial" divisions have limited sci-
        entific interest and may even carry the risk of invit-
        ing abusive generalization.*

    (c) *Current biological knowledge does not permit us to
        impute cultural achievements to differences in ge-
        netic potential. Differences in the achievements of*

different peoples should be attributed solely to their cultural history. The peoples of the world today appear to possess equal biological potentialities for attaining any level of civilization.

Racism grossly falsifies the knowledge of human biology.

In spite of an occasional attempt, by a kind of verbal trickery, to make out that there exist several different living species of man, all authorities agree that all living peoples belong to the same species, *Homo sapiens.* That there are many different peoples who differ physically from one another, and therefore to some extent genetically, is obvious. Such people are often called "races." But we have already made it quite clear that this term is an unfortunate one, and that it were better if it were dropped from common parlance altogether. The variability that characterizes the human species is fascinating, and the differences, far from being made to serve as so many pegs upon which to hang our prejudices, should become points of interest and greater understanding of the manner in which we all came to be the way we are now.

"Racial" classifications, it is pointed out, are of limited scientific interest, and are only too often mistaken for realities which do not in fact exist. Such "realities" are then made to serve as the basis for all sorts of further unjustifiable generalizations. All classifications are more or less arbitrary, and classifications of man are especially so. The danger in all classification is the tendency to forget that it is arbitrary, and no more than a convenience in helping us to deal with refractory materials.

While it is not possible to say with certainty that significant genetic factors do not enter into the differences in cultural achievements of different peoples, the probabilities appear to be very much against such a contingency.[126] What is most probable is that the genes that render cultural achievement possible are *fundamentally similar* in all the populations of humanity. The reason why it is possible to say this with a high degree of probability is that during the several million years or so of man's evolution the selective processes which have been at work on him must have been much the same in all populations.

Throughout the evolutionary history of man he has been a food-gatherer and hunter. It is only during the last 15,000 years of his history that some populations developed agriculture and some went on to develop an urban way of life. All of man's basic potentialities and traits were developed long before that time. Under food-gathering and hunting conditions of life, populations are small and the challenges of the environment, differing as they may from the jungles of central Africa and South America to the icy wastes of the Arctic, remain fundamentally similar. What is required under such conditions of life is the ability to meet the daily demands of life with the necessary adaptive responses. The traits having the highest adaptive value under such conditions are plasticity, malleability, cooperativeness, and the general intelligence which enables the individual to make the most appropriately successful responses to the challenges of the environment. In the course of man's evolution the selective pressures acted not toward the development of any particular ability, but toward the generalized ability of adaptability. Hence, there would have been no development of genetically based special abilities in one population differing from those developed in other groups. Since there was no particular premium placed upon the development of such abilities, there would have been no selection for them in any group.

It is man's generalized ability to adapt himself to all environmental conditions and challenges, *not* a fitness in one special ability or another, which has been at the highest premium in the course of his evolution. It is from such considerations that most anthropologists reason that there exist no significant differences in the genetic constitution for behavior and intelligence as well as for cultural achievement among the various populations of man. Possibly some genetic variability exists for the substrates of behavior as between one population and another, but if such genetic variability does exist it cannot be very large. The variability within populations is almost certainly much greater than that which exists between populations.

To what, then, are due the differences in behavior and cultural achievement that exist among populations? The racist chooses to believe that these differences are due to genes. Anthropologists choose not to believe anything unless there is good evidence for it, and the evidence indicates that, allowing for such genetic variability and its influences to which we have already referred, the behavioral and cultural differences among the populations of mankind are principally, if not wholly, due to the differences in the history of experience of each population. We have already dealt with this matter in discussing the first Statement on Race, but it will be useful here to amplify that discussion.

The peoples of Europe are technologically and in many other respects more advanced than the nonliterate peoples of the world because they have long enjoyed the cross-fertilizing effects of contacts and relations with innumerable peoples of the greatest diversity of cultural background, whereas the nonliterate peoples have been virtually isolated and have not experienced anything resembling the European adventure.

When Caesar landed on the shores of Britain in 55 B.C. he found the inhabitants in a Bronze Age stage of cultural development. The Romans occupied Britain for more than 500 years, then followed the Jutes, the Angles, the Saxons, and the Normans, but it was not before the end of the fifteenth century that the English began to blossom culturally. It took 1500 years of cultural cross-fertilization before the English began to demonstrate what an illiterate people, given sufficient time, should eventually develop. Who, in Roman times, would have thought that they were capable of producing a Shakespeare, a John Donne, a John Keats, a Shelley, a Newton? With a similar history behind them, it is probable that every people could develop along similar lines.

The conditions necessary for the development of a high civilization are very special, and genes or not, there can be no such civilization unless the necessary conditions are present. The same holds true for individual achievement; no matter whether the necessary genes are present or not, there will be no achievement unless the appropriate conditions are present.

On a population basis genius in any high civilization is, in fact, a rare occurrence, while the ability for high achievement is only a little less rare. We cannot speak with certainty of genes for genius in nonliterate populations. It must be remembered that such populations are small, hence the range of variability is likely to be somewhat less for such genes than in a large population. On a population basis one would hardly expect to find genius, although one would expect to find genetic constitutions which, under the appropriate conditions, would be expressed in extraordinarily high achievement. Sequoyah, the Cherokee Indian who from completely nonliterate beginnings invented the Cherokee alphabet and syllabry, represents perhaps the best known example of such a genius, and there have been others. However, one would not expect many geniuses. If there have been such genetic constitutions for genius in nonliterate societies, there has been little call upon them, because there has been no need, and so it is quite possible, even probable, that many geniuses in nonliterate societies have died as mute inglorious Miltons, who were never called upon to pluck the poet's lyre or solve a differential equation. Genius, like high achievement, requires the proper soil in which to flourish. Nor is genius always recognized when it occurs. However, in every society there is no difficulty in recognizing the man of courage, of ability, even though the genes may be there for a great deal more.

Indeed, every bit of evidence available to us indicates that what the average man of any society has done the average man of every other human popoulation can also do. When all the peoples of the world shall have enjoyed all the requisite opportunities and a sufficient amount of time in which to take advantage of them, it will be time enough then to take a census of the distribution of the genes for genius and those for high achievement. At that time, it is to be hoped, such a question will be of merely academic interest, for the really basic question isn't a matter of genes at all, but purely a matter of ethics—neither a matter of science, sociology or skin color, but plainly and simply a matter of humanity.

PARAGRAPH 4

The human problems arising from so-called "race" relations are social in origin rather than biological. A basic problem is racism, namely, antisocial beliefs and acts which are based on the fallacy that discriminatory intergroup relations are justifiable on biological grounds.

Race problems are social problems. Indeed, there are no biological race problems or race problems originating in anything other than social conditions.

It is very important to recognize that what most people understand by "race" represents a social construct, and not a biological fact.

What the social construct says about "race" is that it is a fact that 1) physical appearance based on race, 2) capacity for individual achievement, and 3) capacity for the achievement of high civilization are the three elements that are inseparably biologically linked by "race," and that, therefore, physical appearance based on race is a sufficient condition on which to base dependable predictions concerning the capacity for individual and group achievement of such persons. This is held to be especially true of some peoples like the American Blacks. And the fact is that in such cases it is true. But not for the reason that those holding such views generally give, that is, the biological linkage and determinance of racial appearance, capacity for individual achievement, and capacity for high civilization.

In the first place, there is no biological linkage between genes for racial physical traits, individual ability, and capacity for high civilization. In the second place, where social conditions discriminate against certain "races" it is highly probable that they will show the effects of such discrimination in lower IQ test scores, in lower individual achievement, and as a group in their ability to develop what more advantaged groups call "high civilization." The error committed here is to attribute to biological causes what is in fact due to social conditions. Nevertheless, it is readily seen how easily the biological misinterpretation can become a basis and a justification for discriminatory "race relations."

PARAGRAPH 5

G roups commonly evaluate their characteristics in comparison with others. *Racism falsely claims that there is a scientific basis for arranging groups hierarchically in terms of psychological and cultural characteristics that are immutable and innate. In this way it seeks to make existing differences appear inviolable as means of permanently maintaining current relations between groups.*

While comparisons may be odious, it is nevertheless a common human practice to make comparisons of one's own group with that of others, usually to the disadvantage of the other groups. This is a perfectly understandable form of behavior, but not usually a very productive one. The comparisons made are generally based on insufficient knowledge of the other people, and the conclusions drawn from such comparisons are not, therefore, likely to be either sound or just. Actually, all living peoples have an enormously long history of experience behind them. What has differed in each people's experience to make them somewhat different from each other has been the kind and variety of the challenges, both cultural and physiographic, to which they have been exposed.

Each people has developed the most complex series of responses to the challenges of their particular environments, and to the extent to which those challenges have differed to that extent do the cultures of each people differ.

When we evaluate the qualities of different peoples by the measure of the skill with which they have each adapted themselves to the challenges of their environments, then it becomes perfectly clear that, judged in relation to that skill, every human group has made as good an adaptation as any other. The real question some of us are beginning to ask is whether civilized peoples have really made as successful an adaptation to the challenges of the world in which they live and which, to a large extent, they have created, as the co-called simpler societies.

Certainly there exist societies which are more complex than others. But this difference bears no relation to genetic or innate factors. Food-gathering hunting peoples like the Australian aborigines, for example, may have forms of social organization, kinship systems, and languages which make those of highly civilized societies look primitive. The fact that Australian aborigines wear no clothes, make no hydrogen bombs or nuclear submarines, means only that they have never experienced the need for them, not that they are innately deficient in the genetic potentials which, under the appropriate conditions, would allow them to devise such things. The fact is that we know them to be highly intelligent and gifted people who have become the victims of racist practices, with their land taken from them, their cultures destroyed, and they themselves consigned to the outermost peripheries of White society.[127]

Given adequate opportunities, every people has shown what it can do; that, indeed, there is nothing that any human group has done that any other human group could not also do.

The differences in psychological and cultural characteristics exhibited by different human groups are real, but they are neither innately determined nor immutable. The manner in which peoples have changed in very short periods of time in these respects has been very striking, indeed.

The seafaring Scandinavians of the Bronze Age were undoubtedly the ancestors of the modern Scandinavians, yet
how very different are the sedentary, peaceful, home-re-
forming Scandinavians from their raiding forebears.

The boisterous joy of life of the English in Tudor times
and the lusty libertinism of the Restoration contrast
sharply with the prudery of the Victorian Age. The Englishman's "nature" was different in the sixteenth as compared with that in the seventeenth century, and different
yet again in the nineteenth century.

What did White Americans achieve culturally or by way
of invention up to the War of Independence? Very little,
indeed. "Who reads an American novel," asked an English
wit in the 1840's. Who, indeed? And today who *doesn't*
read an American novel, and acclaim the inventiveness,
the science, and the scholarship of Americans?

And what shall we say of the Jews, who were always described as town-dwellers, addicted to business, and entirely
without the martial qualities so much admired by more
belligerent peoples? In the second half of the twentieth
century, foreign governments send observers to Israel to
learn how to train airmen and soldiers!

How shall we account for the differences in cultural behavior of such biologically near kin as the New Mexican
sedentary Pueblo and the nomadic Navaho Indians, or the
behavior of those inhabitants of Mexican Indian villages
which are completely hispanicized?

Human nature is learned within the limits of each individual's potentialities for being human within a specific
culture. The pattern of behavior known as human nature
is capable of change not only from generation to generation, but in the same person in a single generation.

Racism, with its rigidified separation of peoples into

hierarchies of "races"—"superior" and "inferior" races—creates and erects demeaning barriers between peoples not only where there is not the least justification for them, but which have the negative effect of setting people against one another. And this, apparently, is what racists desire to achieve, for in their opposition to so-called "inferior races" they believe they can best maintain their supremacy. The terms "White suprematicist" and "racist" have the same meaning.

PARAGRAPH 6

F aced with the exposure of the falsity of its biological doctrines, racism finds ever new stratagems for justifying the inequality of groups. It points to the fact that groups do not intermarry, a fact which follows, in part, from the divisions created by racism. It uses this fact to argue the thesis that this absence of intermarriage derives from differences of a biological order. Whenever it fails in its attempts to prove that the source of group differences lies in the biological field, it falls back upon justifications in terms of divine purpose, cultural differences, disparity of educational standards or some other doctrine which would serve to mask its continued racist beliefs. Thus, many of the problems which racism presents in the world today do not arise merely from its open manifestations, but from the activities of those who discriminate on racial grounds but are unwilling to acknowledge it.

The resourcefulness of racists appears to be limitless. An enormous encyclopedia of racist devices and stratagems could be compiled which would constitute a sorry commentary on certain aspects of human character. There have even been scientists who have attempted to show that some human groups are incapable of breeding with one another.[128] There is no truth whatever in such a suggestion, all human groups are mutually interfertile. Reference has been made to this astonishing statement only in order to show how far some racists are willing to go in their anxiety to maintain the separation of peoples.

Racists are usually quite impervious to the disproof of their claims, and it is certainly difficult to dispute such arguments as that if God had wished to create but one "race" He would not have created Blacks and Whites. Anthropologists take the view that differences in skin color represent the end-effect of an adaptive response to long established habitat differences in sunlight intensity. Dark skins originated in high sunlight regions like Africa, and the Tropics in general, while light skins came into adaptive being in the low sunlight regions such as the northern climes.

The disguises under which the less overt forms of racism manifest themselves are legion. Such statements, offered with the appropriate solemnities of expression, as "It is necessary to go slow in attempting to effect improvements in race relations," usually mean either that nothing need be done at all or that slight token gestures may be made, which will amount to much the same thing. "Separate but equal" in the schools as elsewhere represents the typical gloss meaning "the equal right to be separate," and since, in the United States, White parents will frequently choose to have their children "educated" in separate schools, such ritual phrases serve as rationalizations for the maintenance of inequality.

Photographs are often required with applications for employment, and the appropriate discriminations are appropriately made. The stratagems are endless and thoroughly discreditable. It is not only individuals or groups that behave in these ways, but also official bodies and governments.

Racists will stop at nothing, and some of the more active of them have not hesitated to resort to the most discreditable of devices.

PARAGRAPH 7

Racism has historical roots. It has not been a universal phenomenon. Many contemporary societies and cultures show little trace of it. It was not evident for long periods in world history. Many forms of racism have arisen out of the conditions of conquest, out of the justification of Negro slavery and its aftermath of racial inequality in the West, and out. of the colonial relationship. Among other examples is that of antisemitism, which has played a particular role in history, with Jews being the chosen scapegoat to take the blame for problems and crises met by many societies.

It comes as a distinct surprise to most people to learn that the origins of racism are quite recent. Most people, especially those living in racist regions, would be inclined to think that racism was quite an ancient phenomenon. The truth is quite otherwise. Neither among non-literate peoples nor among the peoples of antiquity is there the slightest evidence of anything resembling racism. On the contrary, the evidence points largely in the opposite direction.[129]

The notion that there exist whole groups of mankind who stand in hierarchical relationships of biological superiority or inferiority to one another constitutes a late eighteenth-century early nineteenth-century development—largely growing out of the need to justify the institution and trade in slaves. In order to support slavery, the pro-slavers were compelled to find reasons to show that some men, as Aristotle had said, were born to be slaves while other were born to be masters. The demonstration of the innate, the biological, inferiority of the slaves to their masters seemed to be the best answer to the abolitionists and others who claimed that all men were endowed by the Creator with equal rights to the development of their humanity. It was in this manner that the doctrine of racism was invented and subsequently came to be elaborated.[130] During the second half of the nineteenth century politicians and extreme nationalists began to discover the usefulness of racism, and to find "race" to be a far more effective device than religion, for the achievement of their nefarious purposes. Hitler and the Nazis showed the world how effectively millions of human beings could be murdered in the name of "race." As Hitler remarked in conversation with Hermann Rauschning, "I know perfectly well, just as well as all those tremendously clever intellectuals, that in the scientific sense there is no such thing as race. But you, as a farmer and cattle-breeder, cannot get your breeding successfully achieved without the conception of race. And I as a politician need a conception which enables the order which has hitherto existed on historic bases to be abolished and an entirely new and anti-historic order enforced and given an intellectual basis. . . . With the conception of race National Socialism will carry its revolution abroad and recast the world."[131]

While, as is stated in the paragraph, antisemitism has served racist purposes, it was not originally a racist doctrine in the sense that it was based on biological grounds. On the contrary, it was originally based on alleged differences in culture, religion, behavioral traits, with physical appearance sometimes added as an additionally discriminatory trait.

We repeat once more, racist dogma asserts a trifold correlation of traits biologically linked, namely, 1) biologically determined physical differences in appearance, with which is linked 2) an innate biological constitution characterizing each group, which sets certain limits on the learning abilities of the members of such groups, and 3) likewise sets limits to the ability for cultural achievement of such groups as a whole. This dogma constitutes a very simple explanation of the differences between human groups, and on the face of it constitutes a not unreasonable one. Hence, it has enjoyed an immense popularity among millions of people who, quite understandably, not possessing the knowledge that would enable them to see the falsities of this dogma, accept it as a fact.

The truth is that there is no biological association between external physical traits and individual or group abilities. It is not, in brief, possible to determine from any one of the above-mentioned traits what the genetic or biological potentials may be for any of the others.

The fact that different groups are often characterized not only by differences in physical appearance, but also in the individual behavior of the members of these groups, as well as in their collective behavior in the form of technological, scientific, social, and other achievements, does not mean that there is a biological connection between these traits. Yet that is precisely what racists claim. There is, they assert, a biological connection, and it is this that accounts for the differences between human groups. It is a very easy assumption to make, and it is a very common one. In logic it is known as the fallacy of *post hoc ergo propter hoc,* or the fallacy of false cause, the erroneous conclusion that because things occur together therefore one must be the cause of the other.

The physical differences are, indeed, for the most part genetically determined, adaptive changes, but the differences in the abilities of different groups as well as the differences in the cultural achievements of such groups are almost certainly largely due to differences in opportunities for learning, and to the nature of those opportunities for learning.

PARAGRAPH 8

The anti-colonial revolution of the twentieth century has opened up new possibilities for eliminating the scourge of racism. In some formerly dependent countries, people formerly classified as inferior have for the first time obtained full political rights. Moreover, the participation of formerly dependent nations in international organizations in terms of equality has done much to undermine racism.

The anticolonial revolution of the twentieth century has opened up new possibilities for the development of innumerable peoples who were formerly living under conditions which prevented their full development. Now that so many peoples are free to develop along those lines that they choose for themselves, we are already beginning to see the flourishing of new arts, painting, literature, and social criticism. There are many internal political and social problems which these peoples must solve before many of their citizens will be able to show what they really can do, but in time, given the solution of those problems, we can be confident that they will succeed.

No one has been more impressive at international meetings and organizations than the representatives of newly independent peoples. The presence of such men and women as equals at such organizations may or may not have served to undermine the cause of racism, but with their presence at such events transmitted to the homes of millions of television watchers, an important impact has been made.[132]

PARAGRAPH 9

There are, however, some instances in certain societies in which groups, victims of racialistic practices, have themselves applied doctrines with racist implications in their struggle for freedom. Such an attitude is a secondary phenomenon, a reaction stemming from men's search for an identity which prior racist theory and racialistic practices denied them. None the less, the new forms of racist ideology, resulting from this prior exploitation, have no justification in biology. They are a product of a political struggle and have no scientific foundation.

That the victims of racist practices are sometimes guilty of such practices themselves, constitutes yet another sorry commentary on the confusion into which some people are capable of falling. It is unnecessary to name the many peoples who, at the present time, are engaged in such practices. The saying that every dog must have his underdog constitutes an ancient recognition of a very human failing—the weak attempting to elevate themselves by demeaning and demoting whatever "others" are available for such purposes.

That racism is sometimes produced by racists in the victims of their prejudices, as among many Blacks against Whites, is a perfectly understandable reaction, and constitutes yet another tragic consequence of the effects of racism.

Whether such forms of racism are politically, socially, psychologically, or otherwise motivated, they are on all counts ultimately self-defeating and always individually self-demeaning.

PARAGRAPH 10

*I*n order to undermine racism it is not sufficient that biologists should expose its fallacies. It is also necessary that psychologists and sociologists should demonstrate its causes. The social structure is always an important factor. However, within the same social structure, there may be great individual variation in racialistic behaviour, associated with the personality of the individuals and their personal circumstances.

Racists are, in general, singularly resistant to demonstrations of the falsity of the foundations upon which they base their arguments. One can talk and write endlessly about the facts, that skin color, nose shape, head form, hair form, brain size, and the like are of no significance whatever in determining the behavior of individuals and the cultural achievements of different peoples, without having much effect.

As we have already said, "race" is not a biological problem at all, nor does it present any biological problems which require special attention. "Race" is a problem which is created by special types of social conditions which set people against each other.

The truth is, of course, that it is not the biological differences between peoples that constitute the cause of racist behavior, but certain kinds of social and psychological conditions. It is upon these that the focus of attention is most needed. Certain kinds of societies encourage the development and perpetuation of racism. In such societies the individual may very early in life acquire racist attitudes, and with his fellows grow up to believe that they are perfectly natural and just.[133] The problem is complicated. Much that is called racism isn't that at all. In England for example most of the difficulties called "racial" between whites and colored people are based not on racist attitudes of mind but rather on the general dislike of the foreigner and foreign ways. Differences of any kind, social or physical, may be utilized as a peg upon which to hang one's prejudices. Especially where there is competition for jobs and housing, any kind of group membership difference may be readily seized upon as a target for discrimination and hostility.

The demonstration by psychologists and sociologists of the causes of racism, and its relation to the social structure, while very necessary, will, however, seldom be sufficient to "undermine" the beliefs of most racists. It may serve to "undermine" the beliefs of those who are not racists, but who are merely ill-informed as to the relevant facts. The necessary and sufficient conditions for coping with racism are set out in the paragraphs and their discussion which follow.

PARAGRAPH 11

The committee of experts agreed on the following conclusions about the social causes of race prejudice:
(a) Social and economic causes of racial prejudice are
particularly observed in settler societies wherein are
found conditions of great disparity of power and
property, in certain urban areas where there have
emerged ghettoes in which individuals are deprived
of equal access to employment, housing, political
participation, education, and the administration of
justice, and in many societies where social and economic tasks which are deemed to be contrary to the
ethics or beneath the dignity of its members are assigned to a group of different origins who are derided, blamed, and punished for taking on these
tasks.
(b) Individuals with certain personality troubles may be
particularly inclined to adopt and manifest racial
prejudices. Small groups, associations, and social
movements of a certain kind sometimes preserve
and transmit racial prejudices. The foundations of

> *the prejudices lie, however, in the economic and so-*
> *cial system of a society.*
>
> *(c) Racism tends to be cumulative. Discrimination de-*
> *prives a group of equal treatment and presents that*
> *group as a problem. The group then tends to be*
> *blamed for its own condition, leading to further*
> *elaboration of racist theory.*

Improvement in basic opportunities for everyone, the betterment of living and economic conditions, and better education, will all contribute to the amelioration of intergroup misunderstandings. It is toward the improvement of all these conditions that we must all work rather than on racism itself, for racism is, in the societies in which it flourishes, a reflection principally of the profound inequities and inequalities which prevail in these connections.

While it is true that many persons with certain kinds of personality problems are prone to find racist attitudes toward others congenial to themselves, the problem goes far deeper than that. Men and women who are basically weak and insecure will seek strength and security by joining a group, especially one that is engaged in opposition to some other or others. Drawing vicarious strength from group membership, achieving borrowed strength and identity from identification with such a group, the weak and insecure will not only satisfy this need for membership and recognition by others, but will also achieve a sanctioned target for the accumulated hostility with which the frustrations of life have produced in them.

Such a description, unfortunately, applies to millions of persons, especially in the industrialized socieities of the West. It was seen at work in its most lethal form in Naziism. It is in progress at the present time in South Africa. And although there exists a United Nations and *A Declaration of Human Rights* (see pp. 239-47) and Mr. U. Thant has repeatedly urged the boycott of South Africa until it alters its racist policies of discrimination and repression, neither the member nations of the United Nations nor the signatories to the *Declaration of Human Rights,* with few exceptions, appear ready to implement their words with actions.

a. Social and economic causes of race prejudice are readily seen at work in many societies, and especially so in settler societies, such as the United States and South Africa. These are societies in which one group, the settlers, have imposed their dominance upon the indigenous population or upon others who have migrated into the country, or are of lower socioeconomic status. The disparity of power and property is considerable, and the basic opportunities for growth and development are denied to large segments of the dispossessed population.[134]

Here it is important to understand the meaning of "basic opportunities," and what the denial of these opportunities means for the affected individuals.

In a period when equality of opportunity is a principle which is at long last coming to be widely accepted, it is more than ever necessary to be alerted to certain problems which are bound to develop and which are likely to be with us for some time. Black children, and the children of

Puerto Rican, Mexican, and American Indian descent, as well as others, will increasingly continue to find themselves in schools and in other situations in which they will not, on the whole, do as well as White children. Nor, on the whole, will members of these ethnic groups do as well in the open competitive market as Whites.

In schools and colleges the trend will continue for some time yet among these non-white groups, though to a lesser extent than formerly, to lag substantially behind in IQ tests and in school performance, as well as in general achievement.

In view of these probabilities it is desirable for everyone concerned to understand what that lag almost certainly means, in order to guard against the danger of drawing the wrong conclusions.

Observe, it will be said by many, they (especially Blacks) now enjoy equal opportunities for education, and after years of it, where are their great scientists, their great inventors, their great abstract thinkers? A few writers, yes. Some athletes, yes. But, then, there has always been a sprinkling of those.

Does not this lack of achievement, under condtions of equal opportunity, fully and at long last, remove all doubt that these people are of genetically inferior stuff compared to Whites?

The answer is that while it might seem so, the probabilities are that the failure to achieve equally under conditions of "equal opportunity" is due to environmental rather than to genetic deficiencies. For this conclusion there exists a considerable amount of evidence, some of which we shall consider in what follows. It is, however, much easier to attribute differences in achievement, especially scholastic achievement, to differences in innate factors, to heredity. But since the heredity of the individual represents the expression of the interaction between his genes and the environment in which those genes have undergone development, clearly the environment must always be considered as a major factor in attempting to assess the influences that have been operative in the expression of any trait. The meaning of this statement does not appear to have been always understood by those who have drawn the "obvious conclusions."

There is good reason to believe that what most of us have regarded as "equal opportunities," that is, the process of providing the young of different ethnic groups with the same conditions for learning and intellectual development have, in fact, never existed. Never existed for the simple reason that those opportunities are unequally received. The unequal reception, the evidence suggests, is due not to group genetic differences, but to group cultural differences, to culturally produced impediments in the ability to learn and to think at comparatively equal levels of abstraction.

For high, even adequate, intellectual achievement certain prerequisite conditions are apparently necessary, quite unrelated to the quality of the genetic potentialities of the individual, assuming, of course, that those potentialities are normal. The necessary conditions are complex, but may be described as a stimulating cultural environment which encourages high aspiration levels.

A Black child from the ghetto in the same classroom with a White child from the neighboring White slum areas is not enjoying equal opportunities in the classroom for the simple reason that he is not in a position to learn as relevant to himself much to which he is being exposed. The school generally offers him little that he can creatively incorporate into the background of his own ghetto culture. In that culture respect for learning has no place nor is there any high valuation of the ability for high abstract thought, so necessary for achievement in the sciences, philosophy, and the humanities, not to mention ordinary school work.

The Black ghetto child comes not only from a culture of poverty, but from a poverty of culture, parentally uninspired, rootless, barren, and aridly one-dimensional. He is altogether lacking in a framework in which to fit the ordinates to which he is being exposed, and which are for the most part meaningless to him because he has no means of putting them together into a meaningful coordinate system. The individual himself, it appears, must be rooted in a three- or four-dimensional cultural matrix through the ordinates of which he can meaningfully incorporate, learn, what he is being taught.

It is not sufficiently often pointed out that every individual must learn to learn, and that a great part of this is accomplished by the kind of stimulation he receives in the home, in relationships with parents and siblings, long before the child gets to school. The child, other things being more or less equal, will learn in the school in a manner very largely influenced by the kind of learning experiences he has undergone at home. Here the White child enjoys immense advantages over the Black. By the time the Black child arrives at school he has usually suffered massive deprivations which have resulted not only in a serious failure of development in his learning capacities, but also in his ability to assimilate what he does learn in anything like the meaningful context and manner with which the White child is able to learn.

The kind of changes that must occur in the Black home

and culture before the Black child can enter the classroom on an equal footing with, and as prepared to learn as, the White child are complex. These changes probably belong in the same category as those that are and have been operative in many societies in which peoples of very different cultural backgrounds have come together without the more highly developed one, after many centuries, seeming to have any significant effect in stimulating the creativity of the acculturated group.

Let us consider some examples of this.

The Romans occupied Britain for 500 years, but insofar as any possible stimulus to creativity was concerned the Britons seem largely to have escaped it. Invasions by Scandinavians, Celts, Angles, Jutes, Saxons, and Normans, extending over a period of more than 1000 years, similarly seems to have had little effect. It would, indeed, have been easy to conclude that the Britons were a genetically ill-endowed people. Following all that contact and stimulation by so many different peoples what did the native population have to show for it? An Adam Bede, a Roger Bacon, and the author of *Everyman?* It wasn't much.

And then, all of a sudden, as it were, in the sixteenth century, there was such an explosion of bright stars as the world had not witnessed since the days of Periclean Athens. The appearance of so many major constellations that so unexpectedly illuminated the hitherto virtually empty English firmament: Shakespeare, John Donne, Thomas Heywood, George Chapman, Ben Jonson, Thomas Dekker, Philip Massinger, Christopher Marlowe, Francis Bacon, Gilbert of Colchester, as well as numerous other luminous spirits who followed in a continuous succession of new stellar births, would have been considered highly improbable by most of Britain's conquerors.

It is of interest to note that all these men, including the philosophers and scientists among them, were individuals of outstanding imaginative genius. It was during the second half of the following century, the seventeenth, that there was to develop that equally striking florescence of scientific genius.

From the Roman occupation to the appearance of the first men of genius and high achievement it took 1500 years. This is, of course, a very crass and incomplete statement. A good deal of simmering had undoubtedly gone on for some centuries prior to what appears to have been a sudden explosion of genius. Nevertheless, the fact remains that it was only after 1500 years of acculturative interaction, or whatever it was that was involved, that the English began popping.

It is to be observed that we are speaking here of "high achievement," of "genius." It is by the works of such individuals that we customarily measure a society's or an ethnic group's quality. Apparently certain specific conditions must develop in every culture before the latent potentialities for achievement in each population can be expressed.

What are these necessary specific conditions? These conditions are no longer a matter of conjecture, but on the basis of increasing evidence may be dependably deduced and indicated. The conditions necessary for achievement in any society are: (1) A cultural background of respect for achievement in the family in which the child has been raised. (2) Encouragements and rewards within the family and the culture which make it possible for the individual to acquire whatever is necessary in order for him to achieve in an achieving society. (3) A society in which the conditions of individual development have not physically affected his ability to learn. Nutritional deficiencies, for example, during fetal development may irreversibly damage large numbers of brain cells, and thus seriously affect the child's ability to learn. Nutritional deficiencies during infancy or childhood may produce similar damaging effects.

The effects of some diseases during the early stages of development, prenatal and postnatal, can be equally damaging.

Nutritional deficiencies, especially protein deficiencies, as well as deficiencies induced by disease, are widespread throughout the world, and probably affected whole populations throughout the prehistoric period. This may, at least in part, account for the slow rate of cultural development during the greater portion of man's more than four million years of evolution. During that long period of secular time the struggle to survive constituted a virtually fulltime occupation, and prolonged periods of undernourishment were probably the lot of every individual. Man suffered from protein and vitamin deficiencies, especially ascorbemia, that is, vitamin-C deficiency, a natural deficiency since man lacks the ability to produce vitamin C within his own body and must acquire it mainly from fruits of the citrus variety.

The combination of these factors: (1) the continuous and demanding struggle for existence, (2) the debilitating effects of disease, (3) the neuronally damaging effects of malnutrition would severely limit the members of any population in achieving very much more than was necessary for bare survival. Add to this combination of factors those which continue to exist for many contemporary populations, (4) the absence of any cultural background, and (5) lack of encouragements, rewards, incentives, motivations, and aspirations for extraordinary achievement, and we have the necessary and sufficient conditions for ensuring the nondevelopment of any and all potentialities for extraordinary or even ordinary accomplishment.

Potentialities require the proper environing conditions if they are to grow and develop and find appropriate expression. The expression of any capacity requires opportunities which stimulate the capacities to develop into abilities. Human development is not simply a matter of the unfolding of genetic potentialities but principally a matter of the cumulative, active process of utilizing environmental inputs. The adequate utilization of those inputs depends upon the environmental opportunities afforded the utilizing mechanisms, that is, the genetic potentials. The joker in that pack is, of course, the word "opportunities."

What are "opportunities"? What most culturally developed peoples with masses of nondeveloped people living in their midst have interpreted "opportunities" to mean is the hypocritically simplistic notion that political, legal, and educational rights somehow ensure the freedom to enjoy equal rights in everything else. This is, of course, utter nonsense. The laws on the books assuring equal political, legal, and educational rights to all citizens are, in practice, differentially applied and enforced. Equal laws do not, in practice, work out either as equality before the law or equality of opportunity. Prejudice and discrimination operate to maintain impassable barriers against the subclasses who, as I pointed out many years ago, are treated as members of a lower caste.

In the deprived and depressed conditions under which the members of such subclasses or castes are forced to live they are deprived of the greatest of all opportunities: *the opportunity to learn to respond with advantage to available opportunities.* The absence of this basic opportunity, by whatever means produced, seriously interferes with the ability to respond to the available opportunities.

The *basic opportunity* necessary for all human beings if they are to realize their potentialities is comprised of the obverse of those factors which I have described as principally responsible for the lack of high achievement in the members of certain populations. The necessary ingredients in *basic opportunity* then, necessary for achievement, are: (1) Some freedom from the continuous pressure to survive, that is, the enjoyment of a certain amount of leisure. (2) Good health or relative freedom from disease during fetal and childhood development. (3) Freedom from the effects of malnutrition during fetal, childhood, and adult development. (4) Growth and development in an environment with traditional roots in a cultural background providing the matrix and the context from and in which are derived those meanings which, in terms of those meanings, make the world intelligible and meaningful to the child and the person he becomes. If the traditional roots are deep and extensive, and his cultural background rich and multidimensional, he will have within him what used to be called "an apperceptive mass" which will enable him to respond with advantage to the environment in which he finds himself. If, on the other hand, his traditional roots are shallow or nonexistent and his cultural background arid, he will himself be unable to take root and develop in what remains an essentially inhospitable environment. (5) Finally, for creativity and achievement, the encouragement and nurturing of high aspiration levels, the fueling and development of incentives, the promise and experience of rewards are necessary.

Genius or high achievement remains an unexpressed potentiality in the absence of these conditions. In order to start its motors running not only is the fuel, the opportunities, necessary, but the fuel must be ignited, and that is accomplished not merely by turning the key in the ignition, but by ensuring the presence of an adequately charged battery, *the basic opportunity*. A healthy battery, adequately charged, properly connected to the spark plugs, will respond to the key being turned in the ignition, but not otherwise. All the necessary conditions must be fulfilled if the engine is to be started and to be kept running. It matters not how otherwise well we attend to the design of the car, it will not run unless the basic requirements of its motor are met. So it is with human beings. Unless the basic internal requirements for achievement are met, no matter what external opportunities human beings are exposed to, they will largely be unable to respond to them. The process of achievement is a creative one, creating power by a complex of relations, which are only made possible in an environment of *basic opportunity*.

Most of us are not persons of great or extraordinary achievement, and it is desirable to recognize that in every human context it is not genius in some specific area that is of significance, but rather the generalized ability to make the appropriately successful responses to the ordinary challenges presented by the environment—to be plastic, malleable, and adaptable. And of such adaptive behavior all men everywhere, within the normal range of variation, are capable. Nevertheless, we tend to evaluate the status of societies by the measure of their extraordinary accomplishments. This is fair enough, but it is quite unfair to draw the conclusion from the differences in accomplishment that those which have fewer accomplishments to their credit than others are therefore genetically inferior to the others.

By this measure the Britons would have been held genetically inferior to the Romans. But the truth is they were *not* genetically inferior, but only culturally different, and apparently for the most part quite unmotivated for the very good reason that the conditions of life were such as to be all time-consuming in the struggle for survival. Basic opportunities were almost completely wanting, and it was not until such opportunities were afforded an increasingly large number of individuals in the population that a Shakespeare could make his appearance.

Until similar basic opportunities are afforded all populations compared, whether they be the aborigines of New Guinea or the Blacks of New York, it were premature as well as wholly unjustifiable to attribute differences in achievement between populations to genetic factors.

It is, apparently, difficult to persuade those who are so ready to settle for a genetic explanation of differences in cultural achievement that it is only by equalizing basic opportunities for everyone that the conditions will be provided for making any sort of valid judgments concerning the possible role played by genetic factors in social and individual differences in cultural achievement. Until such basic opportunities are made available to everyone, all statements attributing differences in cultural achievement must be adjudged what they are: conjectures without any scientific basis or merit whatever.

Ultimately, of course, the whole question of "race" is a pseudo one, a system of pseudological rationalizations based on insufficiently analyzed evidence designed, usually, to bolster prejudices and defend indefensible positions, and which at once denies and rejects science, logic and humanity. However unsound and unreal such beliefs may be, we know only too well how very real the unsound and the unreal can become. Be that as it may, it cannot be too often repeated that the issue at stake is not a scientific one, but a question of ethics. By virtue of the fact that he is a human being every individual has a right to his birthright, which is development. The greatest riches of the person of his community, of humanity, lies in the uniqueness of the contribution that each individual has to make to his fellowman.

It is not a question of "superiority" or "inferiority" but the encouragement of individual fulfillment, whatever the individual's limitations, that society must consider among the first of the purposes for which it exists. The greatest of all talents, and the most important for man, is the talent for humanity. And what is talent? It is involvement. And the talent for being humane operationally means the involvement in the welfare of one's fellowman. All human beings have the capacity for such involvement. Racists commit the greatest of all crimes because they obstruct the development of this capacity and prevent the individual's fulfillment as a human being. To the extent that these crimes are committed, to that extent is the individual, society and humanity impoverished.

The deprivation of any man's right to fulfillment diminishes each of us, for we as well as he, have lost what he has been deprived of, for we are all involved in each other. Whether we wish it to be so or not this involvement is inherent in the very nature of nature, and especially of human nature. The most basic of all opportunities is the right to growth and development as a humane being who has been deeply involved in the love of others, for the health and identity of the person consists in the meaningfulness of his interrelationships.

b. While it is true that many persons with personality difficulties fall easily into racist ways of thinking and acting, race prejudice is not by any means limited to individuals with personality problems. Patterns of conformity drilled into normally healthy individuals often lead to patterns of behavioral exclusiveness. Membership in any group often tends to produce a certain discrimination against others. Differences in the others frequently tend to be equated with inferiority of the others.

Such discriminations, however, tend to come into being only in societies in which the social system and the economic organization of society give rise to the conditions which favor such developments. Worries, fears, insecurities, under the appropriate social and economic conditions add up to race prejudice. Hence, it is the social and economic conditions that help to produce racism that must be changed. But even this is not enough, for at the same time we need to educate young people to understand the meaning of humanity. The child acquires attitudes long before he becomes familiar with the facts. Education in humanity may not alone change the world, but it can make a powerful contribution in the right direction. If we would make our human societies more humane, we must begin by making ourselves so. Society is not an abstraction, it is an expression of ourselves.

c. As that great teacher of the young Heinrich Pestalozzi (1746) observed, "He who degrades his fellow man to be a beggar and a knave will always be the first to call him so." Those who deprive others of their right to development are the first to point to the consequences of their own conduct, but, of course, attributing it to the deficiencies of their victims. Not alone this, they tend to blame those whom they have deprived of their rights for their failure to take advantage of them, and adding insult to injury they then go on to attribute the resulting inequalities to innate and irremediable factors. This represents a form of self-fulfilling prophecy, in which by expecting the others to fail, one deliberately withholds the conditions for success, and provides, instead, only those for failure. When the latter are realized, and the predictions and the confidence in one's beliefs are confirmed, what could make a more satisfyingly neat and logical package?

The truth is there is neither reason nor logic involved in such "thinking." What is involved is usually the desire to believe that things are as one believes them to be because this gratifies the need to believe them so. Essentially this is an irrational attitude, and it is the essence of racism that is built on such systems of irrationality. Racists find no difficulty in perpetuating the doctrine of the inequality of races, for most people perceive that there do exist differences between certain populations, and therefore assume that those differences are innately determined. What they frequently fail to see is that those differences, whatever their causes may be, and however the natural inequalities of men in endowment may vary, do not for one moment render equality of opportunity a contemptible principle.

It is because of its denial of equality of opportunity to members of different groups that racism constitutes the repudiation of humanity and the perpetuation of inhumanity, and therefore constitutes one of the worst of all evils.

PARAGRAPH 12

The major techniques for coping with racism involve changing those social situations which give rise to prejudice, preventing the prejudiced from acting in accordance with their beliefs, and combating the false beliefs themselves.

Changing the social situations which give rise to race prejudice, preventing the prejudiced from acting in accordance with their beliefs, and combating the false beliefs themselves, may sound like counsels of perfection that are much easier uttered than carried out. And that is no less than the truth. But it is also no less than the truth that by working to bring about desirable social change such changes can be achieved, that by setting up legal restraints and simple discouragements to racist behavior, the effects, at least, of such behavior can be reduced, and finally, false beliefs can be shown to be what they are.

It will be necessary to be so engaged until such time as we have succeeded in making humane beings out of people. Upon this we shall have more to say.

PARAGRAPH 13

It is recognized that the basically important changes in the social structure that may lead to the elimination of racial prejudice may require decisions of a political nature. It is also recognized, however, that certain agencies of enlightenment, such as education and other means of social and economic advancement, mass media, and law can be immediately and effectively mobilized for the elimination of racial prejudice.

I t was Thomas Mann who remarked "Politics is life." Indeed, it is. It is, therefore, important to understand that politics is one of the best and most effective agencies through which social change may be secured. By the means that are available to every citizen, through his elected representatives, one may bring the necessary pressures to bear that will influnce legislation. By such means individuals as well as organizations have been instrumental in bringing about social change.

It has been said that racial prejudice cannot be legislated out of existence. That may, to some extent, be so, but the practice of racial prejudice can certainly be reduced by legislative means. The fact that the relevant law exists in itself constitutes a social sanction encouraging the nonpractice, at least, of socially undesirable behavior. Furthermore, the law tends to make many people feel comfortable with what it prescribes, and because it is a law they feel compelled to pay attention to it. So let not the power of law be underestimated.[135]

Much more effective use can be made of the mass media, especially television, in combating racism, and in the more enlightened education of everyone concerning the unity of humanity and the value of human relatedness.

PARAGRAPH 14

T*he school and other instruments for social and economic progress can be one of the most effective agents for the achievement of broadened understanding and the fulfillment of the potentialities of man. They can equally much be used for the perpetuation of discrimination and inequality. It is therefore essential that the resources for education and for social and economic action of all nations be employed in two ways:*

(a) The schools should ensure that their curricula contain scientific understandings about race and human unity, and that invidious distinctions about peoples are not made in texts and classrooms.

(b) (i) Because the skills to be gained in formal and vocational education become increasingly important with the processes of technological development, the resources of the schools and other resources should be fully available to all parts of the population with neither restriction nor discrimination;

(ii) Furthermore, in cases where, for historical

reasons, certain groups have a lower average education and economic standing, it is the responsibility of the society to take corrective measures. These measures should ensure, so far as possible, that the limitations of poor environments are not passed on to the children.

In view of the importance of teachers in any educational programme, special attention should be given to their training. Teachers should be made conscious of the degree to which they reflect the prejudices which may be current in their society. They should be encouraged to avoid these prejudices.

(a) Schools should devote far more attention than they have in the past to the education of the young in humanity, in what it means to be a human being, and the manner in which all human beings should be involved in the common enterprise of enabling each other to fulfill their potentialities for love and co-operation.[136] Such an approach would be by far the best toward the elimination of racism, as well as toward the solution of a good many other social problems. Indeed, all education, the central core of education, should be based on a broad foundation of understanding of the meaning of humaneness, of humanity. Anthropology, the science of man, should constitute the central sun of every educational curriculum, around which all other subjects should be taught and integrated. If education is not for humanity, then what is it for? All techniques and skills should be taught and learned in the service of the greater facilitation and enlargement of every human being's ability to fulfill himself in relation to the community of man. Toward this end all teachers should be educated in the fundamentals of anthropology. Indeed, the understandings that anthropology makes possible should be considered the alphabet of education, the alphabet that makes all understandings of human relatedness possible.

(b) (i) Every opportunity for formal and vocational education should be made freely available to everyone, but what should be fully understood is that every individual is unique and is characterized by his own rate of assimilation and learning, so that it is inefficient and unfair and damaging to treat all children in a classroom as if they were all equally capable of learning at the same speed. What is required is not equality of education or equality of treatment, but teaching and opportunities that are equal to the needs of each individual. Equality of opportunity implies an equal right to all the necessary conditions for development, but that should never be taken to mean that all individuals should be treated as if they were members of an undifferentiated agglutinated mass. Every individual is unique, and it is in the fulfillment of his uniqueness that he will make, and should be encouraged to make, his principal contribution to the community of man. Hence, in the community of the classroom, and in the schools, the fact that each represents a microcosmic model of that greater community of the world of man, should be more fully realized and acted out in the everyday relations of its members.

The basic likenesses that exist between human beings are in no way diminished in the endeavor to bring out the unique differences of each. Indeed, the greater the opportunities made available and the more these are adjusted to the needs of the individual, the more fully realized, and in many ways the more differentiated, will each become. At the same time the ability to appreciate the fundamental likenesses in the differences would become the more highly developed. Difference would then be valued not as an occasion for discrimination, but as a privilege of participation in the uniqueness of the others. The shared experience under such conditions would contribute to the greater enrichment of everyone.

(ii) Poor environments make poor people, and poor people make poor children, who then tend to perpetuate the vicious cycle. Everything possible must be done to break this vicious cycle. A responsible society is the reflection of a responsible citizenry, and citizens who have a proper perspective on what the priorities ought to be in the improvement of the human condition, must exercise their right and their obligation to see to it that those priorities receive the attention they deserve.

The importance of teachers, especially in the

schools, in the education of humanity and in the dissolution of racist and otherwise prejudiced attitudes, can hardly be exaggerated. It is especially at these early ages, when attitudes are being formed, that the influence of good teachers can be most effective. Hence, all teachers should be thoroughly grounded in the relevant knowledge and understanding of the facts of anthropology, of race, racism, and the full understanding of the principle that all human beings belong together in the common enterprise of humanity.

The most important communication a teacher can make to his pupil is his own personality. It is, therefore, important that teachers of the young not only be free of the prejudices that may be widespread in their society, but that they themselves be persons who, by caring for their pupils, teach them what caring means and, therefore, how to care for, to be actively involved in, the welfare of others. That kind of teaching in humanity is worth more than all the formal courses put together.

PARAGRAPH 15

Governmental units and other organizations concerned should give special attention to improving the housing situations and work opportunities available to victims of racism. This will not only counteract the effects of racism, but in itself can be a positive way of modifying racist attitudes and behaviour.

Improving the housing conditions and work opportunities for the victims of racism should be a first order priority of every government—local, state, and national. Birth control must be taught, especially in a period in which no one should really have more than two children. That period is now. The emphasis, of course, must be placed on the individual worth of each child, and that, therefore, no more children should be brought into being than we can properly care for. While poverty and disadvantage of every sort are still with us, we must teach people to understand that large families serve only to handicap every member of them, and to deprive them of their individual rights for development. This is especially true in poor and working class families, but at the same time does not for a moment exclude families of the more privileged classes.

Birth control is a recommendation which needs to receive fuller examination and discussion than it has yet received, for what it is concerned with is no less than the liberation of the victims of racism from the conditions which make them the easy marks of the racists. It is, therefore, necessary to emphasize the value of birth control as an agency in the approach to the solution of the problem of racism. The family that is handicapped by too many children is much more likely to be self-defeating than the small family.

PARAGRAPH 16

The media of mass communication are increasingly important in promoting knowledge and understanding, but their exact potentiality is not fully known. Continuing research into the social utilization of the media is needed in order to assess their inflence in relation to formation of attitudes and behavioural patterns in the field of race prejudice and race discrimination. Because the mass media reach vast numbers of people at different educational and social levels, their role in encouraging or combating race prejudice can be crucial. Those who work in these media should maintain a positive approach to the promotion of understanding between groups and populations. Representation of peoples in stereotypes and holding them up to ridicule should be avoided. Attachment to news reports of racial designations which are not germane to the accounts should also be avoided.

The mass media, newspapers, magazines, radio, and especially television can play a very much more substantial role than they do at present in re-educating and educating the people toward a genuine understanding of the relatedness of all human beings to one another.

There is a new image of man emerging in the world, to which television has made a major contribution by bringing the peoples of every part of the world, in their native habitats and out of them, into the living room of the viewer. Representatives of many of these peoples have been seen and heard in interviews, at the United Nations, on panels, and elsewhere. The personalities of these individuals, the charm, high intelligence, and warm humanity, which they frequently exhibit on the television screen, have the most extraordinary effects upon the millions of viewers who, it is most important to note, would remain largely unaffected by exposure to any other means of communication. The repeated shock of recognition experienced in this way has led to the revelation of the fact that the whole world of mankind is, indeed, kin, and that the

so-called "inferior races" are only technologically inferior
to the technologically more developed peoples, to us, and
that given adequate opportunities they are *obviously* capable of producing men and women of high intellectual cali-
ber, and of a humanity which can at least compare favor-
ably with our own. The very expression "inferior race" is
one that would be considered in bad taste by more people
today than would have been thought possible only a few
years ago. To this, without any awareness of the fact that
it was doing so, and without the least propagandistic motivation, television has already made a substantial contribution. While much has been achieved in this enlargement
and enrichment of our image of man, it is little compared
with what could yet be achieved.

It is not merely the image of mankind that requires ren-
ovation. Equally significant is the revision of the person's
self-image which television is capable of working. The potentialities of man are infinitely varied and exciting. But
the image of man and of human potentialities handed
down to us by traditions and traditional ways of setting
limits to individual development often constrict and imprison what is best in man. Today, more than ever, man
stands in need of the stimulation and direction which will
release that "imprison'd splendour" that is within him.

All references to "race," where they are of no relevance
to the matter under discussion, both in conversation and in
the public media, should be avoided, for the very cogent
reason that such references usually serve to reenforce prejudices and contribute to the preservation of stereotypes
which should not be perpetuated.

PARAGRAPH 17

L aw is among the most important means of ensuring equality between individuals and one of the most effective means of fighting racism.

The Universal Declaration of Human Rights of 10 December 1948 and the related international agreements and conventions which have taken effect subsequently can contribute effectively, on both the national and international level, to the fight against any injustice of racist origin.

National legislation is a means of effectively outlawing racist propaganda and acts based upon racial discrimination. Moreover, the policy expressed in such legislation must bind not only the courts and judges charged with its enforcement, but also all agencies of government of whatever level or whatever character.

It is not claimed that legislation can immediately eliminate prejudice. Nevertheless, by being a means of protecting the victims of acts based upon prejudice, and by setting a moral example backed by the dignity of the courts, it can, in the long run, even change attitudes.

To repeat here what has been said earlier: the law can be a most effective means of controlling the practice of race discrimination. Therefore the enactment and enforcement of such laws should, wherever necessary, be encouraged.

The Universal Declaration of Human Rights (see pp. 239-47) of 10 December 1948 sets out in unequivocally clear language the rights and privileges of all human beings everywhere. Each of the thirty articles of the Declaration can be taken as a practical program for conduct applying in every instance from the individual to the international level. These articles should be taught in every school in every land, for what they constitute is a credo for the whole of humanity.

National legislation outlawing any form of racism will not immediately, as we know from the example of the United States, entirely eliminate race prejudice and acts of racial discrimination, but it will certainly create a climate of opinion in which it will be very much easier to bring about the reduction of every form of racism. And this, too, is clearly to be observed in the United States where in many parts of the land fair employment practices, school integration, and open shop unions have resulted in some improvement in the opportunities available to increasing numbers of formerly excluded persons.

Laws that are in any way tainted with racism or are discriminatory must be abrogated. Laws must be instituted which make it impossible for racists to utilize them in the service of racism or to circumvent them.

Is it unrealistic or unreasonable to expect that societies which deny freedom and justice to the poor and the victims of racism will, through changes in the law, bring about changes in the lives of the discriminators and those they discriminate against? The only way in which such a question can be finally answered is by putting it to the test of experience.

It is the values by which people live that determine the ways in which they respond to other people. Hence, it is the values of society that must be constantly examined and, wherever necessary, modified or changed, and adjusted not alone to meet but to encourage and further the development of humane relations between people. If the social context in which the law functions is racist, then the strong tendency will be to use the law to advance racist ends. Clearly, then, the value system of the society will need to be changed, and this can only be accomplished by a combination of approaches involving law, social agencies, the schools, and the church.

PARAGRAPH 18

Ethnic groups which represent the object of some form of discrimination are sometimes accepted and tolerated by dominating groups at the cost of their having to abandon completely their cultural identity. It should be stressed that the effort of these ethnic groups to preserve their cultural values should be encouraged. They will thus be better able to contribute to the enrichment of the total culture of humanity.

The great tragedy that has befallen many peoples has been the loss of their cultural identity. In the attempt to make them acceptable, dominant peoples have often required of the subordinate people that they abandon their traditional ways and adopt those of the dominant culture. Furthermore, many peoples finding themselves in a subordinate position to the "superior" people fall into a posture of subserviency, and wish nothing more than to become like those who dominate them. Soon they come to look upon "the old ways" as inferior, even something of which to be ashamed. In this way the ancient virtues and unique contributions, of religion, folklore, philosophy, language, arts, manufactures, and much else, have been abandoned or rejected and lost.

The fact that whole peoples have been physically exterminated by racists—the Tasmanians by the British, innumerable American Indian tribes by Americans, South American Indian tribes by the Spaniards—and that whole cultures have been deliberately destroyed, and are continuing to be destroyed at the present, by dominant peoples, calls for immediate action on the part of all of us. In Australia, New Guinea, Melanesia, Micronesia, Polynesia, in many parts of Africa, and elsewhere, this destruction is proceeding apace.

The Jews constitute an outstanding example of a people who, through more than 2000 years of living among other peoples have nevertheless maintained their cultural and religious identity, while becoming full and devoted members of the societies in which they have lived and in which they continue to live. Some Jews there have always been who have elected to adopt the cultural identity of the people among whom they have lived, but the majority of Jews have chosen to retain their cultural identity.

What it is necessary to understand is that the greatest riches of mankind lie not only in its genetic diversity but also in its cultural diversity, and that it is far better for humanity to preserve and develop that diversity in living communities than that it be relegated to the display cases of museums.

Dominant peoples should do everything in their power, as a moral obligation, to help and encourage people of other cultures to respect, preserve, and develop their ancestral cultures. This is not in the least incompatible with full membership in the dominant culture and, indeed, in the culture of humanity as a whole.

PARAGRAPH 19

Racial prejudice and discrimination in the world today arise from historical and social phenomena and falsely claim the sanction of science. It is, therefore, the responsibility of all biological and social scientists, philosophers, and others working in related disciplines, to ensure that the results of their research are not misused by those who wish to propagate racial prejudice and encourage discrimination.

The repudiation by scientists and others of the false claims of racists has great importance, in that such denials, when based on the findings of science, make available to the layman the factual evidence for the unity of mankind and the unsupportable claims of racism. The false claims of racists need to be exposed. But urgent as this is, the more important fact will always remain that the unity of mankind while based firmly in the biological history of man rests not upon the demonstration of biological unity, but upon the ethical principle of humanity, which is, to repeat, the right of every human being to the fulfillment of his potentialities as a human being.

APPENDIX

United Nations Universal Declaration of Human Rights

On December 10, 1948, at the Palais de Chaillot, Paris, the General Assembly of the United Nations adopted and proclaimed the Universal Declaration of Human Rights, the full text of which appears in the following pages. Following this historic act the Assembly called upon all Member countries to publicize the text of the Declaration and "to cause it to be disseminated, displayed, read and expounded principally in schools and other educational institutions, without distinction based on the political status of countries or territories."

PREAMBLE

Whereas recognition of the inherent dignity and of the equal and inalienable right of all members of the human family is the foundation of freedom, justice and peace in the world,

Whereas disregard and contempt for human rights have resulted in barbarous acts which have outraged the conscience of mankind, and the advent of a world in which human beings shall enjoy freedom of speech and belief and freedom from fear and want has been proclaimed as the highest aspiration of the common people,

Whereas it is essential, if man is not to be compelled to have recourse, as a last resort, to rebellion against tyranny and oppression, that human rights should be protected by the rule of law,

Whereas it is essential to promote the development of friendly relations between nations,

Whereas the peoples of the United Nations have in the Charter reaffirmed their faith in fundamental human rights, in the dignity and worth of the human person and in the equal rights of men and women and have determined to promote social progress and better standards of life in larger freedom,

Whereas Member States have pledged themselves to achieve, in co-operation with the United Nations, the promotion of universal respect for and observance of human rights and fundamental freedoms,

Whereas a common understanding of these rights and freedoms is of the greatest importance for the full realization of this pledge,

Now, Therefore,

THE GENERAL ASSEMBLY

proclaims

THIS UNIVERSAL DECLARATION OF HUMAN RIGHTS as a common standard of achievement for all peoples and all nations, to the end that every individual and every organ of society, keeping this Declaration constantly in mind, shall strive by teaching and education to promote respect for these rights and freedoms and by progressive measures, national and international, to secure their universal and effective recognition and observance, both among the peoples of Member States themselves and among the peoples of territories under their jurisdiction.

article 1. All human beings are born free and equal in dignity and rights. They are endowed with reason and conscience and should act towards one another in a spirit of brotherhood.

article 2. (1) Everyone is entitled to all the rights and freedoms set forth in this Declaration, without distinction of any kind, such as race, colour, sex, language, religion, political or other opinion, national or social origin, property, birth or other status.
(2) Furthermore, no distinction shall be made on the basis of the political, jurisdictional or international status of the country or territory to which a

person belongs, whether it be independent, trust, non-self-governing or under any other limitation of sovereignty.

article 3. Everyone has the right to life, liberty and security of person.

article 4. No one shall be held in slavery or servitude; slavery and the slave trade shall be prohibited in all their forms.

article 5. No one shall be subjected to torture or to cruel, inhuman or degrading treatment or punishment.

article 6. Everyone has the right to recognition everywhere as a person before the law.

article 7. All are equal before the law and are entitled without any discrimination to equal protection of the law. All are entitled to equal protection against any discrimination in violation of this Declaration and against any incitement to such discrimination.

article 8. Everyone has the right to an effective remedy by the competent national tribunals for acts violating the fundamental rights granted him by the constitution or by law.

article 9. No one shall be subjected to arbitrary arrest, detention or exile.

article 10. Everyone is entitled in full equality to a fair and public hearing by an independent and impartial tribunal, in the determination of his rights and obligations and of any criminal charge against him.

article 11. (1) Everyone charged with a penal offence has the right to be presumed innocent until proved guilty according to law in a public trial at which he has had all the guarantees necessary for his defence.

(2) No one shall be held guilty of any penal offence on account of any act or omission which did not constitute a penal offence, under national or international law, at the time when it was committed. Nor shall a heavier penalty be imposed than the one that was applicable at the time the penal offence was committed.

article 12. No one shall be subjected to arbitrary interference with his privacy, family, home or correspondence, nor to attacks upon his honour and reputation. Everyone has the right to the protection of the law against such interference or attacks.

article 13. (1) Everyone has the right to freedom of movement and residence within the borders of each state.
(2) Everyone has the right to leave any country, including his own, and to return to his country.

article 14. (1) Everyone has the right to seek and to enjoy in other countries asylum from persecution.
(2) This right may not be invoked in the case of prosecutions genuinely arising from non-political crimes or from acts contrary to the purposes and principles of the United Nations.

article 15. (1) Everyone has the right to a nationality.
(2) No one shall be arbitrarily deprived of his nationality nor denied the right to change his nationality.

article 16. (1) Men and women of full age, without any limitation due to race, nationality or religion, have the right to marry and to found a family. They are entitled to equal rights as to marriage, during marriage and at its dissolution.
(2) Marriage shall be entered into only with the free and full consent of the intending spouses.

(3) The family is the natural and fundamental group unit of society and is entitled to protection by society and the State.

article 17. (1) Everyone has the right to own property alone as well as in association with others.

(2) No one shall be arbitrarily deprived of his property.

article 18. Everyone has the right to freedom of thought, conscience and religion; this right includes freedom to change his religion or belief, and freedom, either alone or in community with others and in public or private, to manifest his religion or belief in teaching, practice, worship and observance.

article 19. Everyone has the right to freedom of opinion and expression; this right includes freedom to hold opinions without interference and to seek, receive and impart information and ideas through any media and regardless of frontiers.

article 20. (1) Everyone has the right to freedom of peaceful assembly and association.

(2) No one may be compelled to belong to an association.

article 21. (1) Everyone has the right to take part in the government of his country, directly or through freely chosen representatives.

(2) Everyone has the right of equal access to public service in his country.

(3) The will of the people shall be the basis of the authority of government; this will shall be expressed in periodic and genuine elections which shall be by universal and equal suffrage and shall be held by secret vote or by equivalent free voting procedures.

article 22. Everyone, as a member of society, has the right to social security and is entitled to realization, through national effort and international co-operation and in accordance with the organization and resources of each State, of the economic, social and cultural rights indispensable for his dignity and the free development of his personality.

article 23. (1) Everyone has the right to work, to free choice of employment, to just and favourable conditions of work and to protection against unemployment.

(2) Everyone, without any discrimination, has the right to equal pay for equal work.

(3) Everyone who works has the right to just and favourable remuneration ensuring for himself and his family an existence worthy of human dignity, and supplemented, if necessary, by other means of social protection.

(4) Everyone has the right to form and to join trade unions for the protection of his interests.

article 24. Everyone has the right to rest and leisure, including reasonable limitation of working hours and periodic holidays with pay.

article 25. (1) Everyone has the right to a standard of living adequate for the health and well-being of himself and of his family, including food, clothing, housing and medical care and necessary social services, and the right to security in the event of unemployment, sickness, disability, widowhood, old age or other lack of livelihood in circumstances beyond his control.

(2) Motherhood and childhood are entitled to special care and assistance. All children, whether born in or out of wedlock, shall enjoy the same social protection.

article 26. (1) Everyone has the right to education. Education shall be free, at least in the elementary and fundamental stages. Elementary education shall be compulsory. Technical and professional education shall be made generally available and higher education shall be equally accessible to all on the basis of merit.

(2) Education shall be directed to the full development of the human personality and to the strengthening of respect for human rights and fundamental freedoms. It shall promote understanding, tolerance and friendship among all nations, racial or religious groups, and shall further the activities of the United Nations for the maintenance of peace.

(3) Parents have a prior right to choose the kind of education that shall be given to their children.

article 27. (1) Everyone has the right freely to participate in the cultural life of the community, to enjoy the arts and to share in scientific advancement and its benefits.

(2) Everyone has the right to the protection of the moral and material interests resulting from any scientific, literary or artistic production of which he is the author.

article 28. Everyone is entitled to a social and international order in which the rights and freedoms set forth in this Declaration can be fully realized.

article 29. (1) Everyone has duties to the community in which alone the free and full development of his personality is possible.

(2) In the exercise of his rights and freedoms, everyone shall be subject only to such limitations as are determined by law solely for the purpose of securing due recognition and respect for the rights and free-

doms of others and of meeting the just requirements of morality, public order and the general welfare in a democratic society.

(3) These rights and freedoms may in no case be exercised contrary to the purposes and principles of the United Nations.

article 30. Nothing in this Declaration may be interpreted as implying for any State, group or person any right to engage in any activity or to perform any act aimed at the destruction of any of the rights and freedoms set forth herein.

References

1. Carolus Linnaeus, *Systema Naturae*, Holmiae, Laurentii Salvii, 10th edition, 1758.
2. Charles Darwin, *The Descent of Man*. London: John Murray, 1871, 2 vols. Second edition, 1874; edition of 1901, p. 276.
3. Ibid., p. 270.
4. Ibid., p. 278.
5. R. Ruggles Gates, "Phylogeny and classification of hominoids and anthropoids," *American Journal of Physical Anthropology*, n.s., vol. 2, 1944, pp. 279-92; Raymond Hall, "Zoological subspecies of man at the peace table," *Journal of Mammalogy*, vol. 27, 1946, pp. 358-64; Carleton S. Coon, *The Origin of Races*. New York: Alfred A. Knopf, 1962.
6. Wilfrid E. Le Gros Clark, *Fitting Man to His Environment*. Thirty-First Earl Grey Memorial Lecture, King's College, Newcastle Upon Tyne, England, 1949, p. 19.
7. *Acts* 17:26.
8. Adolph H. Schultz, "Variability in man and other primates," *American Journal of Physical Anthropology*, n.s., vol. 5, 1947, pp. 1-14 Anthony Barnett, *The Human Species*. New York: W. W. Norton, 1950; Frederick S. Hulse, *The Human Species*. New York: Random House, 1971; Theodosius Dobzhansky, *Mankind Evolving*. New Haven: Yale University Press, 1962; C. Loring Brace and Ashley Montagu, *Man's Evolution*. New York: The Macmillan Co., 1965.
9. Harold F. Blum, "Does the melanin pigment of human skin

have adaptive value?" *Quarterly Review of Biology,* vol. 36, 1961, pp. 50-63; C. Loring Brace and Ashley Montagu, *Man's Evolution.* New York: The Macmillan Co., 1965.

10. Ashley Montagu, *Man's Most Dangerous Myth: The Fallacy of Race.* 4th edition. New York: World Publishing Co., 1964; Frederick S. Hulse, "Exogamy and heterosis," *Yearbook of Physical Anthropology,* vol. 9, 1964, pp. 241-57; Frederick S. Hulse, "Ethnic, caste, and genetic miscegenation," *Journal of Biosocial Science,* Supplement, 1, 1969, pp. 31-41; Lionel S. Penrose, "Evidence of heterosis in man," *Proceedings of the Royal Society, B,* vol. 144, 1955, pp. 203-13; David C. Rife, *Hybrids.* Washington, D.C.: Pacific Affairs Press, 1965; Georges Olivier, "Hétérosis et dominance dans les populations humaines, *Comptes rendus de l'Académie des Sciences,* Paris, vol. 259, 1964, pp. 4357-60.

11. Lawrence H. Snyder, "The genetic approach to human individuality," *Science,* vol. 108, 1948, p. 586.

12. Charles Darwin, *On the Origin of Species by Means of Natural Selection; Or the Preservation of Favoured Races in the Struggle for Life.* London: John Murray, 1859, p. 5.

13. Charles Darwin, *The Descent of Man.* London: John Murray, 1874; London, 1904, p. 282.

14. Ashley Montagu (ed.), *Culture and the Evolution of Man.* New York: Oxford University Press, 1962; Ashley Montagu (ed.), *Culture: Man's Adaptive Dimension.* New York: Oxford University Press, 1968.

15. Charles Darwin, *The Descent of Man.* London: John Murray, 1871, 2 vols., pp. 187-88.

16. For an analysis of Darwin's views see Ashley Montagu, *Darwin, Competition, and Cooperation.* New York: Henry Schuman, 1951; also the Introduction to Darwin's *The Descent of Man.* New York: Limited Editions Club, 1971.

17. Thomas Henry Huxley, "The struggle for existence in human society," *The Ninetenth Century* vol. 23, 1888, pp. 161-80.

18. Thomas Henry Huxley, The Romanes Lecture, "Evolution and Ethics," delivered at Oxford 18 May 1893, for which see T. H. and J. S. Huxley, *Touchstone for Ethics.* New York: Harper & Brothers, 1947.

19. Konrad Lorenz, *On Aggression.* New York: Harcourt, Brace & World, 1967; Robert Ardrey, *African Genesis.* New York: Athe-

neum, 1961; Robert Ardrey, *The Territorial Imperative*. New York: Atheneum, 1966; Robert Ardrey, *The Social Contract*. New York: Atheneum, 1970.

20. Ashley Montagu (editor), *Man and Aggression*. New York: Oxford University Press, 1968; Ashley Montagu, *The Direction of Human Development*. Rev. ed. New York: Hawthorn Books, 1970; Leonard Berkowitz, *Aggression: A Social Psychological Analysis*. New York: McGraw-Hill, 1962; J. D. Carthy and F. J. Ebling (eds.), *The Natural History of Aggression*. New York: Academic Press, 1964; John Paul Scott, *Aggression*. Chicago: University of Chicago Press, 1958; S. Garattini and E. B. Sigg (eds.), *Aggressive Behaviour*. New York: John Wiley & Sons, Inc., 1969; Santiago Genoves, *Is Peace Inevitable? Aggression, Violence, and Human Destiny*. New York: Walker and Co., 1970.

21. Paul R. Burkholder, "Cooperation and Conflict Among Primitive Organisms," *American Scientist*, vol. 40, 1952, p. 603.

22. Ashley Montagu, (ed.), *Culture and the Evolution of Man*. New York: Oxford University Press, 1962; See the Introduction, Ashley Montagu (ed.), *Culture and the Evolution of Man*. New York: Oxford University Press, 1962.

23. For the further development of this viewpoint see Petr Kropotkin, *Mutual Aid*. New York: Doubleday & Co., 1902; William Patten, *The Grand Strategy of Evolution*. Boston: Badger, 1910; Warder C. Allee, *Cooperation Among Animals*. New York: Henry Schuman, 1951; Warder C. Allee, *Animal Aggregations*. Chicago: University of Chicago Press, 1931; Ashley Montagu, *The Direction of Human Development*. Rev. ed. New York: Hawthorn Books, 1970; Ashley Montagu, *On Being Human*. New York: Hawthorn Books, 1969; Ashley Montagu, *Darwin, Competition, and Cooperation*. New York: Henry Schuman, 1951; T. A. Goudge, *The Ascent of Life*. London: Allen & Unwin, 1961; C. H. Waddington, *The Ethical Animal*. New York: Atheneum, 1960.

24. V. Gordon Childe, *Social Evolution*. New York: Henry Schuman, 1951, p. 176.

25. See Ashley Montagu (ed.), *Culture: Man's Adaptive Dimension*. New York: Oxford University Press, 1968; see also note 23.

26. William W. Krauss, "Race Crossing in Hawaii," *Journal of Heredity*, vol. 32, 1941, pp. 371-78; Newton E. Morton, Chin S.

Chung, and Ming-Pi Mi. *Genetics of Interracial Crosses in Hawaii.* New York: Karger, 1967.

27. Ernst Mayr, *Systematics and the Origin of Species.* New York: Columbia University Press, 1940, p. 120.

28. Theodosius Dobzhansky, "On species and races of living and fossil man," *American Journal of Physical Anthropology,* n.s., vol. 2, 1944, pp. 251-56.

29. Ashley Montagu, *An Introduction to Physical Anthropology.* 3rd ed., C C Thomas, Springfield, Ill., 1961; James N. Spuhler, "An estimate of the number of genes in man," *Science,* vol. 198, 1948, p. 279; Robley D. Evans, "Quantitative inferences concerning the genetic effects of radiation on human beings," *Science,* vol. 109, 1949, pp. 299-304.

30. Stanley M. Garn, *Human Races.* 3rd ed. Springfield, Ill.: C C Thomas, 1970.

31. Carleton S. Coon, *The Origin of Races.* New York: Alfred A. Knopf, 1962.

32. For further reading in anthropology see Ashley Montagu, *Man: His First Two Million Years.* New York: Columbia University Press, 1969; C. Loring Brace and Ashley Montagu, *Man's Evolution.* New York: The Macmillan Co., 1965; Clyde Kluckhohn, *Mirror for Man.* New York: Whittelsey House, 1949; Marvin Harris, *Culture, Man, and Nature.* New York: Thomas Y. Crowell, 1971.

33. Caroline B. Day, *A Study of Some Negro-White Families in the United States.* Cambridge, Mass.: Peabody Museum, Harvard University, 1932; Ruggles R. Gates, *Pedigrees of Negro Families.* Philadelphia: The Blakiston Company, 1949.

34. Most anthropologists prefer to speak of "nonliterate" peoples rather than of "primitive" peoples. The term "primitive" implies an early stage of development. Since this introduces a confusing element into the understanding of any people who have not developed a system of writing it is preferable to describe them by a term referring to this fact. See Ashley Montagu (ed.), *The Concept of the Primitive.* New York: Free Press, 1968.

35. See Andrew D. Weinberger, "A Reappraisal of the Constitutionality of 'Miscegenation' Statutes," in Ashley Montagu, *Man's Most Dangerous Myth: The Fallacy of Race.* New York: World Publishing Co., 4th ed. 1964, pp. 402-26.

36. See note 33 and Robert P. Stuckert, "African Ancestry of the White American Population," *The Ohio Journal of Science*, vol. 58, 1959, pp. 155-60; T. Edward Reed, "Caucasian Genes in American Negroes," *Science*, vol. 165, 1969, pp. 762-68.

37. For the rates of intermarriage between Blacks and Whites, see Joseph R. Washington Jr., *Marriage in Black and White*. Boston: Beacon Press, 1970; Albert I. Gordon, *Intermarriage*. Boston: Beacon Press, 1964; Milton M. Gordon, *Assimilation in American Life*. New York: Oxford University Press, 1964.

38. Julian H. Lewis, *The Biology of the Negro*. Chicago: University of Chicago Press, 1942; Caroline B. Day, ref. 33; Ashley Montagu, "Myths Relating to the Physical Characters of the American Negro," in *Man's Most Dangerous Myth: The Fallacy of Race*, pp. 291-316; Otto Klineberg (ed.), *Characteristics of the American Negro*. New York: Harper & Brothers, 1944.

39. Melville J. Herskovits, *The American Negro*. New York: Alfred A. Knopf, 1928; Melville J. Herskovits, *The Anthropometry of the American Negro*. New York: Columbia University Press, 1930; Jack C. Trevor, "Race Crossing in Man," *Eugenics Laboratory Memoirs*, vol. 36, 1953, p. iv + 45.

40. By *genetic equilibrium* is meant the condition of a population in which successive generations consist of the same genetic structure or genotype with the same frequencies, in respect of particular genes or arrangements of genes. See Max Levitan and Ashley Montagu, *Textbook of Human Genetics*. New York: Oxford University Press, 1971.

41. See Ashley Montagu, (ed.), *The Concept of Race*. New York: Free Press, 1964; Jean Hiernaux, "Adaptation and Race," in *Advancement of Science* 1967, pp. 658-62; Jean Hiernaux, "Biological Aspects of the Racial Question," in *Four Statements on the Race Question*. Paris: UNESCO, 1969, pp. 9-16.

42. Earl C. Kelley, *Education for What is Real*. New York: Harper & Brothers, 1947; Hadley Cantril, *The "Why" of Man's Experience*. New York: The Macmillan Co., 1950; Floyd Matson and Ashley Montagu, (eds.), *The Human Dialogue*. New York: Free Press, 1967; James G. Martin, *The Tolerant Personality*. Detroit: Wayne State University Press, 1964; Theodosius Dobzhansky, *The Biology of Ultimate Concern*. New York: New American Library, 1967.

43. For good discussions of the Jews see Maurice Fishberg, *The Jews*. New York: Charles Scribner's Sons, 1911; Karl Kautsky, *Are the Jews a Race?* New York: International Publishers, 1926; Melville J. Herskovits, "Who are the Jews?" in *The Jews: Their History, Culture, and Religion,* Louis Finkelstein ed., 2 vols., New York: Harper & Brothers, 1949, pp. 1151-71; Erich Kahler, *The Jews Among the Nations*. New York: Frederick Ungar, 1967; Roger Kahn, *The Passionate People*. New York: William Morrow and Co., Inc., 1968; Louis A. Berman, *Jews and Intermarriage*. New York: Thomas Yoseloff, 1968.

44. For further discussion of the Jews along these lines see Ashley Montagu, "Are the Jews a race?" in *Man's Most Dangerous Myth: The Fallacy of Race*. New York: World Publishing Co., 4th ed., 1964, pp. 317-38.

45. For a luminous discussion of this see Erich Kahler, *The Jews Among the Nations*. New York: Frederick Ungar, 1967.

46. UNESCO, *Race and Science*. New York: Columbia University Press, 1961. Containing the eleven brochures issued by UNESCO on the various aspects of race.

47. Ashley Montagu, (ed.), *The Concept of Race*. New York: Free Press, 1964. For the critical examination of the concept of race and its inadequacies.

48. J. S. Huxley and A. C. Haddon, *We Europeans*. New York: Harper & Brothers, 1936, pp. 82-83.
In which the term "race" is rejected and the argument for "ethnic group" is first stated.

49. W. T. Calman, *The Classification of Animals*. New York: John Wiley & Sons, 1949, pp. 14-18. An excellent discussion of the meaning of classification.

50. Hans Kalmus, *Genetics*. London: Penguin Books, p. 45, 1948.

51. Hans Kalmus, *Variation and Heredity*. London: Routledge, 1957, p. 30.

52. G. S. Carter, *Animal Evolution*. New York: The Macmillan Co., 1951, p. 163.

53. Ernst Hanhart, "Infectious Diseases," in Arnold Sorsby (ed.), *Clinical Genetics*. St. Louis, Mo.: The C. V. Mosby Co., 1953, p. 545.

54. Lionel S. Penrose, "Review," *Annals of Eugenics,* vol. 17, 1952, p. 252.

55. J. P. Garlick, "Review," *Annals of Human Genetics*, vol. 25, 1961, pp. 169-70.

56. Raymond E. Hall, "Zoological Subspecies of Man at the Peace Table," *Journal of Mammalogy*, vol. 27, 1946, pp. 358-64.

57. A. E. Housman, *The Name and Nature of Poetry*. New York: Cambridge University Press, 1933, p. 31.

58. Henry E. Sigerist, *A History of Medicine*, vol. 1. New York: Oxford University Press, 1951, p. 101.

59. George Gaylord Simpson, *The Major Features of Evolution*. New York: Columbia University Press, 1953, p. 268.

60. Alfred Korzybski, *Science and Sanity*. 2nd ed. Lancaster, Pa.: Science Press, 1941, 31.

61. Horace B. English and Ava C. English, *A Comprehensive Dictionary of Psychological and Psychoanalytical Terms*. New York: Longmans, 1958, p. 189.

62. L. L. Bernard, *Instinct: A Study in Social Psychology*. New York: Holt, 1924.

63. William James, *The Varieties of Religious Experience*. New York, Longmans, 1902, p. 148.

64. Otto Klineberg, "Mental Testing of Racial and National Groups," in *Scientific Aspects of the Race Problem* (ed. by J. W. Corrigan), New York: Longmans, 1941.

65. Arthur B. Jensen, "How Much Can We Boost IQ and Scholastic Achievement?" *Harvard Educational Review*, vol. 39, 1969, pp. 1-123; Lee Edson, "Journalism, *n*. The Theory that IQ is Largely Determined by the Genes." *The New York Times Magazine*, 31 Aug. 1969, pp. 10-11, 40-41, 43-47.

66. J. McVicker Hunt, *Intelligence and Experience*. New York: Ronald Press Co., 1961.

67. Berkev S. Sanders, *Environment and Growth*. Baltimore: Warwick & York, 1934; Herbert G. Birch and Joan D. Gussow, *Disadvantaged Children: Health, Nutrition, and School Failure*. New York: Harcourt, Brace & Jovanovich, 1970; Martin Deutsch and Associates, *The Disadvantaged Child*. New York: Basic Books, 1967; Rodger Hurley, *Poverty and Mental Retardation*. New York: Random House, 1969; Sonia F. Osler, and Robert E. Cooke, *The Biosocial Basis of Mental Retardation*. Baltimore: The Johns Hopkins Press, 1965; Frank Riessman, *The Culturally Deprived Child*. New York: Harper & Row, 1962.

68. H. H. Davidson, *Personality and Economic Background*. New York: King's Crown Press, 1943; J. McVicker Hunt, *The Challenge of Incompetence and Poverty*. Urbana: University of Illinois Press, 1970.

69. M. Deutsch, I. Katz, and A. R. Jensen (eds.), *Social Class, Race, and Psychological Development*. New York: Holt, Rinehart & Winston, 1968; K. Ells, et al., *Intelligence and Cultural Differences*. Chicago: University of Chicago Press, 1951; Ashley Montagu, *Man's Most Dangerous Myth: The Fallacy of Race*. New York: World Publishing Co., 4th ed., 1964.

70. Paul György and O. L. Kline (eds.), *Malnutrition Is a Problem of Ecology*. New York: Karger, 1970.

71. See notes 68 and 69.

72. Walter F. Bodmer and Luigi L. Cavalli-Sforza, "Intelligence and Race," *Scientific American*, vol. 223, 1970, pp. 19-29.

73. Harry F. Harlow, "The Formation of Learning Sets," *Psychological Reviews*, vol. 56, 1949, pp. 51-65; Harry F. Harlow, "Learning and Satiation of Response in Intrinsically Motivated Complex Puzzle Performance by Monkeys," *Journal of Comparative and Physiological Psychology*, vol. 43, 1958, pp. 289-94.

74. W. R. Thompson and W. Heron, "The Effects of Restricting Early Experience on the Problem-Solving Capacity of Dogs," *Canadian Journal of Psychology*, vol. 8, 1954, pp. 17-31.

75. Urie Bronfenbrenner, "Early Deprivation in Mammals: A Cross-Species Analysis," in G. Newton and S. Levine, eds., *Early Experience and Behavior*, Springfield, Illinois: C C Thomas, 1968, pp. 627-764.

76. Edward L. Bennett, Mark R. Rosenzweig, and Marian C. Diamond, "Rat Brain: Effects of Environmental Enrichment on Wet and Dry Weights," *Science*, vol. 163, 1969, pp. 825-26; Mark R. Rosenzweig, David Krech, Edward L. Bennet, and Marian C. Diamond, "Modifying Brain Chemistry and Anatomy by Enrichment and Impoverishment of Experience," in Grant Newton and Seymour Levine (eds.), *Early Experience and Behavior*. Springfield, Illinois: C C Thomas, 1968, pp. 258-98.

77. N. D. Henderson, "Brain Weight Increases Resulting From Environmental Enrichment: A Directional Dominance in Mice." *Science*, vol. 169, 1970, pp. 776-78.

78. R. J. Light and P. V. Smith, "Social Allocation Models of In-

telligence," *Harvard Educational Review,* vol. 39, 1969, pp. 484-510; A. L. Stinchcombe, "Environment: The Cumulation of Events," *Harvard Educational Review,* vol. 39, p. 511-22.

79. Otto Klineberg, *Social Psychology.* New York: Holt, Rinehart & Winston, Inc., 1954.

80. J. H. Rohrer, "The Test Intelligence of Osage Indians," *Journal of Social Psychology,* vol. 16, 1942, pp. 99-105.

81. T. R. Garth, "A Study of the Foster Indian Child in the White Home," *Psychological Bulletin,* vol. 32, 1935, pp. 708-9.

82. R. M. Cooper, and J. P. Zubek, "Effects of Enriched and Restricted Early Environments on the Learning Ability of Bright and Dull Rats," *Canadian Journal of Psychology,* vol. 12, 1958, pp. 159-64.

83. Erwin Ackerknecht, "White Indians," *Bulletin of the History of Medicine,* vol. 15, 1945, pp. 15-36; Howard H. Peckham, *Captured By Indians.* New Brunswick, New Jersey: Rutgers University Press, 1954.

84. Amram Scheinfeld, *Your Heredity and Environment.* New York and Philadelphia: J. B. Lippincott, 1965, pp. 624-25.

85. There are innumerable such persons in the American population.

86. For a beautiful and sympathetic account of the Australian aborigines see Eleanor Dark's novel *The Timeless Land,* New York: The Macmillan Company, 1941. For a full scientific account see Ronald M. and Catherine H. Berndt, *The World of the First Australians.* Chicago: University of Chicago Press, 1964. On the kind of cultural "exposure" which white peoples afford "native" peoples, see A. Grenfell Price, *White Settlers and Native Peoples,* New York: Cambridge University Press, 1950.

87. See "Race and Culture," in Ashley Montagu's *Man's Most Dangerous Myth: The Fallacy of Race.* New York: World Publishing Co., 4th ed., 1964, pp. 238-51; Anne Anastasi, *Differential Psychology.* New York: The Macmillan Co., 4th ed., 1958.

88. For a fuller development of these ideas see Theodosius Dobzhansky and Ashley Montagu, "Natural Selection and the Mental Capacities of Mankind," *Science,* vol. 105, 1947, pp. 587-90.

89. D. Efron, *Gesture and Environment.* New York: Columbia University Press, 1941.

90. Howard F. Peckham, *Captured By the Indians.* New Brunswick,

New Jersey: Rutgers University Press, 1954.

91. Margaret Mead, *Sex and Temperament in Three Primitive Societies*. New York: Delta Books, 1950.

92. Ruth Benedict, *Patterns of Culture*. New York: Mentor Books, 1946; Douglas Haring (ed.), *Personal Character and Cultural Milieu*. Syracuse, N.Y.: Syracuse University Press, 1956; Clyde Kluckhohn, Henry A. Murray, and David M. Schneider (eds.), *Personality in Nature, Society, and Culture*. New York: Alfred A. Knopf, 1953; Bert Kaplan, *Studying Personality Cross-Culturally*. Evanston, Illinois: Row, Peterson & Co., 1961; John J. Honigmann, *Personality in Culture*. New York: Harper & Row, 1967; Victor Barnouw, *Culture and Personality*. Homewood, Illinois: Dorsey Press, 1963; Ralph Linton, *The Cultural Background of Personality*. New York: D. Appleton-Century Co., 1945; J. S. Slotkin, *Personality Development*. New York: Harper & Brothers, 1952; Francis L. K. Hsu (ed.), *Aspects of Culture and Experience*. New York: Abelard-Schuman, 1954.

93. Hamilton Fyfe, *The Illusion of National Character*. London: Watts & Co., 1946; Ernest Barker, *National Character*. London: Methuen & Co., 4th ed., 1948; John Oakesmith, *Race and Nationality*. New York: Frederick A. Stokes, 1919; Friedrich Hertz, *Nationalism*. London: Routledge, 1944; Friedrich Hertz, *Race and Civilization*. London: Kegan Paul, 1928; Friedrich Hertz, *Nationality in History and Politics*. London: Kegan Paul, 1944; Oscar Handlin, *Race and Nationality in American Politics*. Boston: Little, Brown & Co., 1957.

94. Otto Klineberg, H. A. Fjeld, and J. P. Foley, Jr., "An Experimental Study of Personality Differences Among Constitutional, 'Racial,' and cultural groups," reported and discussed in Anne Anastasi and John P. Foley, Jr., *Differential Psychology*, New York, The Macmillan Company, 1949, pp. 746-86; Thomas R. Garth, *Race Psychology*. New York: Whittlesey House, 1931, pp. 156-75; Margaret Anderson, *The Children of the South*. New York: Farrar, Straus & Giroux, 1966; Mary F. Greene and Orletta Ryan, *The Schoolchildren*. New York: Pantheon Books, 1965; Judith R. Kramer and Seymour Leventman, *Children of the Gilded Ghetto*. New Haven: Yale University Press, 1961; Abram Kardiner and Lionel Ovesey, *The Mark of Oppression*. New York: W. W. Norton, 1951; Kenneth Clark, *Dark Ghetto*, New York: Harper & Row, 1965.

95. Helen H. Davidson, *Personality and Economic Background.* New York: Kings Crown Press, 1943; Anne Anastasi, *Differential Psychology.* New York: The Macmillan Company, 3rd ed., 1958; E. L. Thorndike, *Human Nature and the Social Order.* New York: The Macmillan Company, 1940; Raymond W. Mack (ed.), *Race, Class, and Power.* New York: American Book Co., 1963; Philip Mason, *Patterns of Dominance.* New York: Oxford University Press, 1970.

96. Gordon W. Allport, *Personality.* New York: Holt, 1937, p. 469; Gordon W. Allport, *Personality and the Social Encounter.* Boston: Beacon Press, 1960; Clyde Kluckhohn, *Mirror for Man.* New York: Whittlesey House, 1949, pp. 102-44; Abraham Maslow, *Motivation and Personality.* New York: Harper & Row, 1970.

97. C. Loring Brace and Ashley Montagu, *Man's Evolution.* New York: The Macmillan Company, 1965.

98. See "The Creative Power of 'Race' Mixture," in Ashley Montagu's *Man's Most Dangerous Myth: The Fallacy of Race.* New York: World Publishing Co., 4th ed., 1964, pp. 185-223.

99. Julian H. Lewis, *The Biology of the Negro.* Chicago: University of Chicago Press, 1942; S. J. Holmes, *The Negro's Struggle For Survival.* Berkeley: University of California Press, 1937.

100. See note 98.

101. Cedric Dover, *Half-Caste.* London: Secker & Warburg, 1937; Everett V. Stonequist, *The Marginal Man; A Study in Personality and Culture Conflict.* New York: Charles Scribner and Sons, 1937.

102. William E. Castle, "Biological and Social Consequences of Race Crossing," *American Journal of Physical Anthropology,* vol. 9, 9, 1926, p. 149.

103. Anne Anastasi, *Differential Psychology.* New York: The Macmillan Co., 3rd ed., 1958.

104. Ashley Montagu, "Intelligence of Northern Negroes and Southern Whites in the First World War," *American Journal of Psychology,* vol. 58, 1945, pp. 161-88.

105. Based on materials in note 104.

106. F. L. Marcuse and M. E. Bitterman, "Notes on the Results of Army Intelligence Testing in the First World War," *Science,* vol. 104, 1946, pp. 231-32.

107. J. Lawrence Angel, "Social Biology of Greek Culture Growth,"

American Anthropologist, vol. 48, 1946, pp. 493-533; J. Lawrence Angel, "A Racial Analysis of the Ancient Greeks," *American Journal of Physical Anthropology,* vol. 2, n.s., 1944, pp. 329-76.

108. *To Secure These Rights: The Report of the President's Committee on Civil Rights.* U. S. Government Printing Office, Washington, D.C., 1947; L. Bryson, L. Finkelstein, and R. M. McIver (eds.), *Approaches to Group Understanding.* New York: Harper & Brothers, 1947; Kurt Lewin, *Resolving Social Conflicts,* New York: Harper & Brothers, 1948; Peter I. Rose, *The Subject Is Race.* New York: Oxford University Press, 1968; Joseph P. Witherspoon, *Administrative Implementation of Civil Rights.* Austin, Texas: University of Texas Press, 1968; Charlotte Epstein, *Intergroup Relations for Police Officers.* Baltimore: Williams & Wilkins, 1962; Alfred J. Marrow, *Living Without Hate.* New York: Harper & Brothers, 1951; Lillian Smith, *Now Is The Time.* New York: Viking Press, 1955; Margaret Mead and James Baldwin, *Rap on Race.* New York & Philadelphia: J. B. Lippincott, 1971; Peter Goldman, *Report From Black America.* New York: Simon & Schuster, 1971; William L. Taylor, *Hanging Together: Equality in an Urban Nation.* New York: Simon & Schuster, 1971; Basil Davidson, *The African Genius.* Boston: Little, Brown and Co., 1969.

109. Samuel Lowy, *Man & His Fellow Men.* London: Kegan Paul, 1944.

110. See pp. 239-47 of the present volume.

111. See p. 241 of the present volume.

112. Sidney Hook, "Naturalism and Democracy, in *Naturalism and the Human Spirit* (ed., Y. H. Krikorian), New York: Columbia University Press, 1944, pp. 40-64.

113. Warder C. Allee, *Animal Aggregations.* Chicago: University of Chicago Press, 1931; Warder C. Allee, *Cooperation Among Animals.* New York: Henry Schuman, 1951; Ashley Montagu, *The Direction of Human Development.* Rev. ed. New York: Hawthorn Books, 1970; Ashley Montagu, *On Being Human.* 2nd ed. New York: Hawthorn Books, 1969.

114. Patrick Geddes and J. A. Thomson, *The Evolution of Sex.* London: Scott, 1889; Petr Kropotkin, *Mutual Aid.* New York: Doubleday, 1901; A. V. Espinas, *Des Sociétés animales.* Paris, Bal-

lière, 1878, 3rd ed., 1924; Louis O. Katsoff, *The Design of Human Behavior*. St. Louis: Educational Publishers, 1953; William Patten, *The Grand Strategy of Evolution*. Boston: Badger, 1920. For further references see Ashley Montagu, *The Direction of Human Development*. Rev. ed. New York: Hawthorn Books, 1970, pp. 353-55.

115. Warder C. Allee, "Where Angels Fear to Tread: A Contribution From General Sociology to Human Ethics," *Science*, vol. 97, 1943, p. 521.

116. Note 115.

117. Chauncey D. Leake, "Ethicogenesis," in *Studies in the History of Science and Learning* (ed., Ashley Montagu), New York: Henry Schuman, 1946, pp. 262-75; Chauncey D. Leake and Patrick Romanell, *Can We Agree?* Austin: University of Texas Press, 1950.

118. Paul Burkholder, "Cooperation and Conflict Among Primitive Organisms," *American Scientist*, vol. 40, 1952, p. 603.

119. For a fuller development of these views see Ashley Montagu, *On Being Human*. New York: Hawthorn Books, 2nd. ed., 1969; Ashley Montagu, *The Direction of Human Development*. New York: Hawthorn Books, 1970; Ashley Montagu, *The Human Revolution*. New York: Bantam Books, 1967.

120. Note 119 and Abraham Maslow, *Motivation and Personality*. New York: Harper & Row, 1970.

121. Roderick Gorney, *The Human Agenda*. New York: Simon & Schuster, 1972; Ashley Montagu, *The Direction of Human Development*. Rev. ed. New York: Hawthorn Books, 1970.

122. Charles Darwin. *The Descent of Man*. London: John Murray, 1871.

123. John Donne, Seventeenth Devotion, In *Complete Poetry and Selected Prose* (ed., John Hayward), London: The Nonesuch Press, 1929, p. 538.

124. Ashley Montagu, *On Being Human*. New York: Hawthorn Books, 2nd ed., 1969.

125. Ronald Segal, *The Race War*. New York: Viking, 1967.

126. Kenneth Mather, *Human Diversity*. New York: Free Press, 1965; Alexander Alland, *Human Diversity*. New York: Columbia University Press, 1971.

127. Alan Moorehead, *The Fatal Impact*. New York: Harper & Row,

1966; Douglas Lockwood, *We, the Aborigines.* Melbourne: Cassell Australia, 1963; Douglas Baglin and David R. Moore, *People of the Dreamtime: The Australian Aborigines.* New York: Walker and Company, 1970; Charles Mountford, *The Aborigines and Their Country.* New York: Humanities Press, 1969; Mary D. Miller and Florence Rutter, *Child Artists of the Australian Bush.* London: Harrap, 1952.

128. R. Ruggles Gates, *Human Ancestry.* Cambridge: Harvard University Press, 1948, p. 368.

129. Aubrey Diller, *Race Mixture Among the Greeks Before Alexander.* Illinois Studies in Language and Literature, vol. 20, University of Illinois, Urbana, 1937; T. J. Haarhoff, *The Stranger at the Gate.* New York: The Macmillan Co., 1948; H. C. Baldry, *The Unity of Mankind in Greek Thought.* New York: Cambridge Unversity Press, 1965.

130. Thomas F. Gossett, *Race: The History of an Idea.* Dallas, Texas: Southern Methodist University Press, 1963; Ashley Montagu, *The Idea of Race.* Lincoln, Nebraska: The University of Nebraska Press, 1963.

131. Hermann Rauschning. *The Voice of Destruction.* New York: G. P. Putnam's Sons, 1940, p. 232.

132. See "Television and the New Image of Man," in *The Human Dialogue* (eds. Floyd W. Matson and Ashley Montagu), New York: Free Press, 1967, pp. 355-62.

133. Gordon W. Allport, *The Nature of Prejudice.* Cambridge: Addison-Wesley, 1953; Raymond W. Mack (ed.), *Prejudice and Race Relations.* Chicago: Quadrangle Books, 1970; Kenneth B. Clark, *Prejudice and Your Child.* Boston: Beacon Press, 1955; UNESCO, *Race and Science.* New York: Columbia University Press, 1961; Charles Y. Glock and Ellen Siegelman (eds.), *Prejudice U. S. A.* New York: Praeger, 1969; Ashley Montagu, *Man's Most Dangerous Myth: The Fallacy of Race.* New York: World Publishing Co., 4th ed., 1964.

134. A. Grenfell Price, *White Settlers and Native Peoples.* New York: Cambridge University Press, 1950; V. G. Kiernan, *The Lords of Creation.* Boston: Little, Brown, 1969; Philip Mason, *Patterns of Dominance.* New York: Oxford University Press, 1970; Louis L. Snyder (ed.), *The Imperialism Reader.* Princeton, N.J.: Van Nostrand, 1962; René Maunier, *The Sociology of Colonies: An*

Introduction to the Study of Race Contact. 2 vols. London: Routledge, 1949; Winthrop D. Jordan, *White Over Black: American Attitudes Toward the Negro 1550-1812.* Chapel Hill, N.C., University of North Carolina Press, 1968.

135. Morroe Berger. *Equality By Statute.* New York: Doubleday, 2nd ed., 1967.

136. Ashley Montagu. *The Direction of Human Development.* New York: Hawthorn Books, 1970.

For Further Reading

ACKERMAN, NATHAN W., and MARIE JAHODA. *Anti-Semitism and Emotional Disorder*. New York: Harper & Brothers, 1950.

A psychoanalyst and a social psychologist combine to throw light on the character of the kind of persons who indulge in antisemitism. The examination of the motivations of such persons is exemplified by the report on persons undergoing psychoanalysis.

ADORNO, T. W., E. FRENKEL-BRUNSWIK, D. J. LEVINSON, and R. N. SANFORD. *The Authoritarian Personality*. New York: Harper & Brothers, 1950.

A classic work on the origins, development, and nature of the prejudiced person. The book is based entirely upon the cooperative researches of the authors, and is the most exhaustive and thorough study of its kind.

ALLAND, ALEXANDER. *Human Diversity*. New York: Columbia University Press, 1971.

An up-to-date, clear, and effective discussion of the origins and significance of human diversity.

ALLPORT, GORDON W. *The Nature of Prejudice*. Cambridge, Mass.: Addison-Wesley, 1953.

A fine study of the motivations and dynamics of the prejudiced and their prejudices.

BANTON, MICHAEL. *Race Relations*. New York: Barnes & Noble, 1968.
A very readable and thorough analysis of race relations.

BANTON, MICHAEL. "Social Aspects of the Race Problem," in *Four Statements on the Race Question*. Paris and New York: UNESCO, 1969, pp. 17-29.
An excellent discussion.

BETTELHEIM, BRUNO, and MORRIS JANOWITZ. *Dynamics of Race Prejudice*. New York: Harper & Brothers, 1950.
A psychological and sociological study of race prejudice as exhibited by a cross-section of American veterans of World War II living in a large American city.

BONGER, WILLEM A. *Race and Crime*. New York: Columbia University Press, 1943.
An authoritative examination of the relation between race and crime.

COHN, NORMAN. *Warrant for Genocide: The Myth of the Jewish World Conspiracy and the Protocols of the Elders of Zion*. London: Eyre & Spottiswoode, 1967.
A revealing and important study of the sinister forces that have been at work in the geneisis and perpetuation of antisemitism.

COLES, ROBERT. *Children of Crisis: A Study of Courage and Fear*. Boston: Little, Brown, 1967.
On the environment in which the Black child is forced to live in the Southern States. An illuminating work.

COOK, JAMES GRAHAM. *The Segregationists*. New York: Appleton-Century-Crofts, 1962.
Defiance of the 1954 Supreme Court decision on integration in the South.

COUDENHOVE-KALERGI, HEINREICH. *Anti-Semitism Through the Ages*. London: Hutchinson, 1935.
An authoritative study.

DAHLBERG, GUNNAR. *Race, Reason and Rubbish: A Primer of Race Biology*. New York: Columbia University Press, 1942.

An excellent discussion, in genetical terms, of race and the fallacies of racism.

DARK, ELEANOR. *The Timeless Land.* The Macmillan Co., 1941. This is a magnificent novel, but it also achieves perhaps the most sympathetic and authentic insight into the mind of a nonliterate people, in the present case, of the Australian aborigines.

DAVIDSON, BASIL. *The African Past.* Boston: Little, Brown & Co., 1964.
A fine book on African civilizations of the past.

DOBZHANSKY, THEODOSIUS. *Mankind Evolving.* New Haven: Yale University Press, 1962.
A splendid study of the evolution of the variety of man.

JOHN DOLLARD. *Caste and Class in a Southern Town.* New Haven: Yale University Press, 1937.
A classic work on the dynamics of race prejudice in the Deep South.

DUMOND, DWIGHT L. *America's Shame and Redemption.* Marquette, Michigan: Northern Michigan University Press, 1965.
An eloquent and moving discussion of race relations in America by a distinguished scholar.

DUNN, LESLIE C., and THEODOSIUS DOBZHANSKY, *Heredity, Race, and Society.* New York: Mentor Books, 1946.
A valuable discussion of race and race problems by two distinguished geneticists.

FINOT, JEAN. *Race Prejudice.* Los Angeles: Zeitlin and Ver Brugge, 1906.
Published in 1906, this book is still available and remains one of the best books ever published on race prejudice.

FRANKLIN, JOHN HOPE (ed.). *Color and Race.* Boston: Houghton Mifflin Co., 1968.
A valuable series of contributions on the role of color in race prejudice.

FRANKLIN, JOHN HOPE. *From Slavery to Freedom: A History of American Negroes.* New York: Alfred A. Knopf, 1961.

A fine history of Blacks in America.

FRAZIER, FRANKLIN E. *The Negro in the United States.* New York: Macmillan Co., 1949.

An encyclopedic, and very readable, sociological account of the American Negro.

FREDERICKSON, GEORGE M. *The Black Image in the White Mind.* New York: Harper & Row, 1971.

Subtitled "The Debate on Afro-American Character and Destiny, 1817-1914," this is an invaluable history of the origins of contemporary racism in America. Important and highly readable.

FRIEDMAN, LEON. (ed.), *The Civil Rights Reader.* New York: Walker & Co., 1968.

Basic speeches and documents relating to the contemporary civil rights movement.

GINZBERG, ELI, and ALFRED S. EICHNER. *The Troublesome Presence.* New York: Free Press, 1964.

The record of discrimination against the American Negro.

MARY ELLEN GOODMAN. *Race Awareness in Young Children.* Cambridge, Mass.: Addison-Wesley, 1952.

An excellent discussion of the development of race attitudes in children.

GORDON, ALBERT I. *Intermarriage.* Boston: Beacon Press, 1964.

A valuable sociological study of intermarriage.

GOSSETT, THOMAS F. *Race: The History of an Idea.* Dallas, Texas: Southern University Methodist Press, 1963.

An excellent exposition of the origin and development of the idea of race.

GREBLER, LEO, JOAN W. MOORE, and RALPH C. GUZMAN. *The Mexican-American People.* New York: Free Press, 1970.

A splendid study of America's second largest minority group.

GRIER, WILLIAM H., and PRICE M. COBBS. *Black Rage.* New York: Basic Books, 1968.

Two black psychiatrists tell the story "like it is" behind the black man's justifiable anger.

HAARHOFF, T. J. *The Stranger at the Gate.* New York: The Macmillan Co., 1948.
An admirable study of the attitudes of the peoples of classical antiquity toward other peoples.

HANNERZ, ULF. *Soulside: Inquiries Into Ghetto Culture and Community.* New York: Columbia University Press, 1970.
A magnificent study of the Black ghetto in Washington, D.C.

HELPER, ROSE. *Racial Policies and Practices of Real Estate Brokers.* Minneapolis: University of Minnesota Press, 1969.
A sociologist takes a close look at the basic problems underlying discrimination in housing.

HERSCH, JEANNE (ed.). *Birthright of Man.* New York: Unipub Inc., 1969.
Issued by UNESCO this splendid volume presents a panorama of human aspirations toward liberty and freedom, in proverbs, charters, declarations, poems, legal documents, great books, and the like. An impressive, moving, and indispensable volume.

HERTZ, FRIEDRICH. *Race and Civilization.* London: Kegan Paul, 1928.
A splendid work.

HUXLEY, JULIAN S., and ALFRED C. HADDON. *We Europeans.* New York: Harper & Brothers, 1936.
Two distinguished scientists, a biologist and an anthropologist, here offer one of the best analyses of race and racism yet written. This is the work in which it was first suggested that the term "race" be dropped from the vocabulary and "ethnic group" substituted for it.

ISAAC, JULES. *The Teaching of Contempt: The Christian Roots of Anti-Semitism.* New York: Holt, Rinehart & Winston, 1964.
A most enlightening work.

JACKSON, HELEN H. *A Century of Dishonor: A Sketch of the United States Government's Dealings With Some of the*

Indian Tribes. New York: Harper & Brothers, 1881. Reprinted by Harper & Brothers, 1965.

A famous book retailing the atrocious record of the U.S. Government in its dealings with its Indian wards.

JORDAN, WINTHROP D., JR. *White Over Black.* Chapel Hill: University of North Carolina Press, 1968.

A fine study of the dominance of Whites over Blacks in America.

KAHLER, ERICH. *The Jews Among the Nations.* New York: Frederick Ungar, 1967.

One of the best books ever written on the Jews.

KELSEY, GEORGE D. *Racism and The Christian Understanding of Man.* New York: Charles Scribner's Sons, 1965.

An analysis and Christian criticism of racism as an idolatrous religion.

"The Kerner Report." *Report of the National Advisory Commission on Civil Disorders.* New York: Bantam Books, 1968.

A splendid official report on racism and its consequences in America.

KLINEBERG, OTTO. *Race Differences.* New York: Harper & Brothers, 1936.

A standard work on what is known of race differences.

KLUCKHOHN, CLYDE. *Mirror for Man.* New York:

An excellent introduction to general anthropology and the science of human relations. Especially good on race and racism.

KNOWLES, LOUIS L. and KENNETH PREWITT (eds.). *Institutional Racism in America.* Englewood Cliffs, N.J.: Prentice-Hall, 1969.

On the institutionalized racist practices of America.

KOZOL, JONATHAN. *Death At An Early Age.* Boston: Houghton Mifflin Co., 1967.

The destruction of the hearts and minds of Black children in the Boston schools.

Loye, David. *The Healing of a Nation*. New York: W. W. Norton, 1971.
An admirable psychological and sociological study of racism in America, with an original program for political and social reform.

Malcolm X. *Autobiography*. New York: Grove Press, 1965.
One of the great autobiographical accounts of what it is like to grow up black in America.

Mason, Philip. *Common Sense About Race*. New York: The Macmillan Co., 1961.

Masuoka, Jitsuichi, and Preston Valien (eds.), *Race Relations: Problems and Theory*. Chapel Hill, N.C.: University of North Carolina Press, 1961.
Nineteen essays on race relations in mid-century.

Mendelson, Wallace. *Discrimination*. Englewood Cliffs, N.J.: Prentice-Hall, 1962.
A résumé of the five-volume report on the United States Commission on Civil Rights by the editor-in-chief of the 1961 *Report*.

Newby, I. A. *Challenge to the Court: Social Scientists and the Defense of Segregation, 1954-1966*. Baton Rouge: Louisiana State University Press, rev. ed., 1969.
A magnificent book, with responses by some of those criticized.

Olson, Bernhard E. *Faith and Prejudice*. New Haven: Yale University Press, 1963.
On the relation between Christian teaching in the churches and race prejudice.

Porter, Judith D. R. *Black Child, White Child*. Cambridge: Harvard University Press, 1971.
A fine research study on the development of racial attitudes in Black and White children. There are some excellent suggestions for the handling of the problems presented.

Shibutani, Tamotsu, Kian M. Kwan, and Robert H. Billigmeier. *Ethnic Stratification: A Comparative Approach*. New York: The Macmillan Co., 1965.

An excellent study of ethnic stratification as a part of the more complex processes and problems of social differentiation.

SILBERMAN, CHARLES E. *Crisis in Black and White*. New York: Random House, 1964.
A bold and profound attempt to understand the meaning of the Black-White crisis in America.

STEINER, STAN. *La Raza: The Mexican Americans*. New York: Harper & Row, 1970.
A vivid and significant book.

STEINER, STAN. *The New Indians*. New York: Harper & Row, 1969.
On the rise of a new awakening among American Indians.

THOMPSON, EDGAR R. and EVERETT C. HUGHES (eds.). *Race: Individual and Collective Behavior*. New York: Free Press, 1958.
An admirable and most readable reader on race.

TUCKER, FRANK H. *The White Conscience*. New York: Frederick Ungar, 1968.
The White man placed on the analyst's couch. A most searching and stimulating book.

UNESCO. *Research on Race Relations*. New York: Unipub Inc., 1966.
Authoritative surveys on race and race relations in Africa, America, Asia, Europe, and Oceania, by twelve experts.

UNESCO. *Some Suggestions on Teaching About Human Rights*. New York: Unipub Inc., 1968.
A most helpful little book.

VAN DEN BERGHE, PIERRE L. *Race and Racism: A comparative Perspective*. New York: John Wiley, 1967.
A fine comparative study.

WEINBERG, MEYER (ed.). *Integrated Education*. Beverly Hills, California: The Glencoe Press, 1968.
A valuable reader.

Index